About

Abena P. A. Busia is an As[...]
of Literatures in English [...]
Rutgers, The State University of New Jersey, [...]
taught since 1981. Born in Accra, Ghana, she spent the first
years of her childhood at home, as well as in Holland and
Mexico before her family finally settled in Oxford, England,
where she read for a BA in English Language Literature at St
Anne's College, Oxford in 1976, and a DPhil in Social
Anthropology (Race Relations) at St Antony's College in 1984.

She is co-editor, with Stanlie M. James, of *Theorizing Black
Feminisms: The Visionary Pragmatism of Black Women* and of
Beyond Survival: African Literature & the Search for New Life,
publications from the proceedings of the 1994 African
Literature Association Conference, with Kofi Anyidoho and
Anne V. Adams. She lectures and has published widely on
literature of the Black world, and curriculum transformation
of race and gender. She is also co-ordinator and co-editor with
Tuzyline Jita Allan, and Florence Howe of the Feminist Press of
Women Writing Africa; a multi-volume continent-wide publish-
ing project of cultural reconstruction. Her poetry has been
published in various magazines and anthologies in West
Africa, North America and Europe and her volume of poems,
Testimonies of Exile was published by Africa World Press,
Trenton, New Jersey in 1990.

About the Book:
In Abena Busia's mesmerising reflections, vibrant life flows
into the confusions of memory bringing meaning, that we may
hope to be at peace with the eternal.

– Esi Sutherland-Addy, Head of the Language,
Literature & Drama Section, Institute of African Studies,
University of Ghana, Legon.

Traces
of a
Life

A Collection of Elegies and Praise Poems

Abena P.A. Busia

An Adinkra symbol meaning
Ntesie maternasie
A symbol of knowledge and wisdom

Ayebia Clarke Publishing Limited gratefully acknowledges Arts Council SE Funding

Copyright © 2008 *Traces of a Life: A Collection of Elegies and Praise Poems* Abena P. A. Busia
Copyright © 2008 of publication by Ayebia Clarke Publishing Ltd.

First published in English in the UK by Ayebia Clarke Publishing Ltd.
7 Syringa Walk
Banbury
OX16 1FR
Oxfordshire
UK

Distributed in Africa, Europe and the UK by TURNAROUND Publisher Services at www.turnaround-uk.com

Distributed outside Africa, Europe and the United Kingdom exclusively by Lynne Rienner Publishers, Inc.
1800 30th Street, Ste. 314
Boulder, CO 80301
USA
www.rienner.com

Co-published in Ghana with the Centre for Intellectual Renewal
56 Ringway Estate, Osu, Accra, Ghana.
www.cir.com

British Library Cataloguing-in-Publication Data.

Cover design by Amanda Carroll at Millipedia.
Cover artwork by Petra Börner / www.dutchuncle.co.uk
Typeset by FiSH Books, Enfield, Middlesex.
Printed and bound in Great Britain by CPI Cox & Wyman, Reading, Berkshire.

ISBN 978-0-9555079-7-7

Available from www.ayebia.co.uk or email info@ayebia.co.uk
Distributed in Africa, Europe and the UK by TURNAROUND at www.turnaround-uk.com

To Akos, My Sister, & The People
Whose Lives These Poems Have Traced.

Contents

Introduction

By Véronique Tadjo

In our part of the world, saying goodbye to the departed is a careful and lengthy process. Ritual occupies centre stage and the many ceremonies in honour of the Dead bring the whole community together.

The African oral tradition is powerful and at no point is it more moving than when it attempts to restore the memory and dignity of the beloved who have departed. Words are uttered, whispered in silence, libations poured and prayers given to the Ancestors so they can welcome into their realm those who are about to cross the big River.

We may be modern people who rely on technology, individuals who travel the world, intellectuals who hold high degrees, when death knocks at the door, everything is reassessed. It is the nature of our spiritual being, that anguish is the driving force of our experience on earth.

At the beginning of writing, there is always this interrogation about our genealogy, our past. Generation after generation, we ask the same question: do we still have a future? What is our inheritance?

With a greater awareness of the past comes a better capacity to organise the present and plan for tomorrow.

Words have the power to conquer death. Language can awaken vital forces; renew their strength, even if for a fleeting moment. To memorise the passing of time, fix its collective weight in the sacred language of the drums, or in the words of the story-tellers, the royal court historians or the poetry of praise-singers.

But evolving, adapting to the flow of life, this oral tradition was permanently told and retold with an *old newness* that allowed it to cross centuries. So that thoughts would not evaporate. So that good deeds would not be forgotten. So that people who have lived and suffered would not die in vain.

Abena Busia's new collection of poems, *Traces of a Life...* is steeped in this long tradition. She is a contemporary praise-singer, who rises when a solemn occasion demands a poem or words of recognition from the community. She speaks in a voice that has renewed the genre.

> *So come, eat, you who marched the trail of tears and died here;*
> *You, the rebellious and you, the weak,*
> *come, eat, you whose spirits were broken by the flesh markets*
> *   and the forts;*
> *you, the heroic and you the conspirators,*
> *come, eat, you who tried to just make a way to live, and faltered.*
>
> *You of unnameable ancestors, and unknown descendants, come*
> *Here, after all, you are safe.*
> *Here every Friday and every Monday*
> *one woman at a time, through the centuries, has prayed for you,*
> *has fed you milk under a baobab tree scarred by your iron*
> *and swathed in calico to greet you through the centuries*
> *unwitnessed, unacknowledged, unmemorialised.*

By taking central stage, when the community is in need of reassurance and soothing, she restores African women's voices to the public sphere. Hers is a rewriting of history through poetry.

With a clear consciousness about her responsibility in society, the poet prepares the ground for young people by giving them role models while showing them the path taken by their predecessors.

A sense of loss permeates the collection; loss in all its dimensions. The knowledge that life is but transitory and that we must cherish the moments of joy that cross our lives; memories of friends, relatives, the much loved Father.

we can not
comprehend
why every day
we feel
bereaved
anew

Having an acute sense of time, Abena Busia carefully dates her poems, like dots on the map of existence, precise moments threatened by oblivion.

She talks to us like friends, drawing us into her world. Words behind invisible words.

Testament For The First Accused, written as a homage to Nelson Mandela's twenty-seven years in jail, reminds us that in the chaos that is life, the speed at which our destinies collide, somewhere, someone made a difference for all of us. The poem's leitmotiv *For you were still alive, And you were still not free* is reminiscent of a dirge or a lament.

This is where Abena Busia's awareness of history and its tortuous path is evident. She does not idealise Mandela, even going as far as pointing out that in spite of his great sacrifice, we are the ones who are still not free. The poem has a Pan African dimension:

After twenty-seven years of fighting, marching, and singing
We keep a ninety-minute watch;
To see you take these next few steps
On this your No Easy Walk
To our uncertain Freedom;
To witness your release into this changing world,
Unceasingly the same.
For you are still alive,
But we are still not free.
Amandla, Mandela
A Luta Continua!

God versus Nothingness. The poet's mind oscillates between the two. Faced with suffering and personal loss, her faith quivers. The death of a child is harrowing.

Words Fail.
Those of us who love you agonise in advance
Over the inadequate language of sorrow

And

At the moment of hesitation before the knife falls,
we are both Abraham and Isaac
trapped:

this razor's edge of human choice
is all we ever had.

Births and rejoicing are also part of this collection of poems, in the same way as they are part of life in its entirety. A mother's love and tenderness; the comfort of friendship, the fond memories of childhood are all there and this is what brings us hope.

What matters is the journey that makes dark places bright.

Véronique Tadjo
Johannesburg, July 2008.

Preface

Abena P. A. Busia

The impetus for putting together these poems as a *collection* (as opposed to the writing of the individual pieces) comes from a chance remark made by my sister, Akosua, in 1998. I had just read her the poem, over the phone, 'Of Memory and Loss' that I had written for the twentieth anniversary of our father's passing. I was the child present at the ceremony of the unveiling of the headstone, twenty years too late, who had been asked by my siblings to say something on their behalf, as that last task was a filial responsibility and our duty to perform. When she heard the poem, my sister, much moved, grew quiet and then said: "You know, Abe, this seems to be your gift. You managed to say for us what we want to say and can't find the words for. Have you ever thought of collecting those poems all together?" At that point, I had not, so this collection is dedicated to my sister, Akosua, for giving me the impetus to draw together the many poems I had written over the decades. A handful of these poems appeared many years ago in my first collection, *Testimonies of Exile* (AWP, Trenton NJ, 1990), but very few. Though some of the poems were written before the publication of that volume, they were not published there. Most have been written since.

On the poems of loss

Although I do not have access, in writing, to either of my natal languages, I still consider myself, by tradition, a Ghanaian poet – or more precisely, a praise poet, a modern *griót*. Grióts are trained oral historians, and unifiers – key figures, in West African society in particular, who carry the cultural knowledge and identity of each people. Variously described as 'spokespersons, ambassadors, masters of ceremony, tutors, praise-singers, historians, genealogists, musicians, composers, town-criers, and exhorters of troops about to go into battle' (Bowles and Hale, 1996: 77), they occupy a variety of places in the social landscape from master court historians to gossips, depending on the community. Though the real art of linguistic dexterity in Akan or Ga (my father and mother tongues) are closed to me, I consider myself as having access to those ordinary, everyday traditions of linguistic ritual that give rise to poetic form. And I also know myself to be somebody who lives a Diasporic existence, with access to other African Diasporic cultures and the writings and expressive forms they support. To borrow Stephanie Newell's appellation, I consider myself amongst those "grióts with pens in their hands". (Newell, 2006: 124)

Of my natal tradition, it is well known in West Africa that when one thinks of the form 'ritual dirges', one thinks of 'Akan dirges'. The peoples of Ghana, in particular the Akans have long established poetic traditions of ritual mourning, including dirges and praise poems for the deceased. Such poems celebrate the legacy and lineage of that person, whose life history and experiences are marshalled, called together, as a way of explaining who they were and their greatness on the path they trod on this earth. Who they were and what they did is always put in the context of the connections they made and the legacies they left behind. And this is a form that is recognisable and understood and, of course, as is the case with most obituaries, adulatory.

Thus it is in a sense no surprise, culturally speaking, that at moments of distress and mourning, I turn to the poetic form. In *Testimonies of Exile*, the poem "Exiles" is the first I ever wrote about mourning. It is not included in this collection because it is not a testimonial poem to a *particular* person but it is my first expression of witness to what mourning means, particularly for those of us in exile; the inability to grieve in the forms in which we know to be familiar. However, when I started writing poetry during those exile years, the larger cultural context of ritual mourning poetry was unknown to me – that only became clear over the years. At the time I wrote the first two poems in this collection – for my cousin who died two weeks after my twenty-first birthday and for Max Yergan, a friend of my father's whose funeral was the first I had ever attended – I had no concept that I was writing within a tradition; or if I did, the tradition is not the one I now identify myself with so strongly: it was one I had learned, if you like, through the Wordsworthian elegy; or the "Terrible Sonnets" of Gerard Manley Hopkins. Not to say either that these were my conscious designs; simply that they were the first clues I had to the possibility of poetry evoking a sense of sacred mourning.

Over the years, I moved away from the idea of the Wordsworthian and Hopkins Sonnets and much closer to the notion of a ritual calling of the name of the mourned one through the act of libation pouring. Thus a poem such as my tribute to Audre Lorde is much closer to that notion of a collective ritual which *summons up* the spirit of the person being addressed, rather than one meant for private consolation, lamenting the fact that the person is no longer present. The invocation of the spirit of the person lies at the heart of West African traditional ritual mourning.

Although mine are written poems, the idea behind most of them is the context of public shared oral performance and ritual; and in fact, many of the poems were written for public performance and testimonial. They were for the most part, written to be shared rather than to be recorded private moments of personal solace or secret joys. Some of them already had a public space to be shared when written, some of them did not; but the nature of their inscription carried a consciousness of that potential. Again, this has been a process, and the poem that marks the start of the journey is 'Testimonies for Father'. I came to its stanzas slowly in the thirty months or so following father's death, and it was first read publicly by my mother on the fifth anniversary of his passing. But more significantly, for my sense of the place of ritual poetry, that there could be such a journey was propelled by friends of mine: having heard me perform the poem in non-ritual spaces, such as the African Literature Association Conference, they read it out at the funerals of their own fathers, paying me the honour both of selecting the poem and talking about why they had chosen to do so. That is to say, the poems moved out of private spaces into the public spaces in which they belong, the shared public spaces of collective mourning. I am trying to chart the slow transformation of my awareness of a context for the poems that should always have been, but in truth rather *grew* to be, familiar.

On the poems of shared laughter

Like all collections, the combined experience of these poems is both random and precise, like the bric-a-brac of someone with deliberate, but selected tastes. I have found shocks to be harder to encompass than surprises; each death appears singular to each of us and impacts as such, whereas laughter is easier to share than tears, and each birth or other triumphant celebration seems more obviously communal. Thus what these poems struggle with is that contradiction: that ritually speaking, in the end, shared laughter is more singular, single grief more communal. Each death is felt by each of us in a particular way, yet each person shares in a common grief of a lost loved one through modes of mourning, (at least in Ghana) that reflect on death as communal, to be borne collectively. Rituals of mourning are more readily available to share than those of laughter, which has few ceremonials.

All people mourn, and all of us celebrate. What matters, and what changes, is the way we do these things. These poems are deliberate in that sense. Each of them is an 'occasional' poem in the sense of being written for a particular occasion of grief or celebration. There has been too much mourning of late, and the elegies began to outnumber the praise poems; it is perhaps that season of our lives, or at least of my life. The praise poems come out of that shared common space of public celebratory poetry, though the early ones, in terms of form ("Silver Wedding", "For Lennon Who Will Never Be Sixty Four") are less invested in West African ritual antecedents, less conscious in the writing, of the strategies of assemblage shared by the later praise poems and the elegies. For me, in terms of composition, the line between the praise poems for the living and those for the dead becomes increasingly slight. For they too, like elegies and obituaries, gather together the elements of the life being celebrated, and what I invoke in the praise poems is indeed references to those same elements of life in the contexts in which they touched mine. This is most true of those poems written specifically for celebratory purposes such as "Ring Shout for the Ancestors" for Sterling Stuckey and "Titles for Wesley Brown: Take Two", for these poems are assembled from those elements of their lives that mattered for that occasion. The one to Wesley Brown is almost entirely composed of the titles of, or echoes to, his written works, and that to Sterling Stuckey is full of allusions and references to those articles of his that shaped my own work, and to things and people he celebrated, from Paul Robeson to Thelonious Monk, including the echo of a line from a poem by his mother. Were the poems to be performed to music as custom would have it, what would be most dramatically different between the two groups is not necessarily the shape of the poems themselves, but the sound of the accompanying music and the mode of performance. What they all share is the cultural recognition of the ritual power of story in poetry to celebrate a friend, and acknowledge the life and works of those people with whom you have shared your life.

On the organisation of this collection

Once the poems were assembled together, it was natural to think of them in their categories of "elegies" and "praise poems", and when preparing the manuscript for sending to the editor, that is, in fact, how they were initially arranged. The elegies were grouped together and the praise poems were also grouped together, one after the other. Something did not ring true. The reason for the falsity was obvious, to me at least – I realised that that this is not the way I had lived my life or experienced the events that I was, through those poems, commemorating. My friends did not die all at once, nor did they get married or give birth all at once. As happens in life, the events were juxtaposed against each other; a wedding anniversary can come shortly after a funeral; a retirement dinner shortly after a memorial service. It therefore became clear what should have been self-evident: that the poems needed to be arranged chronologically in the order of events. That is to say, in the order in which they had been experienced. Once this was done, it gave rise to the title of the collection: when the poems were extracted from the isolated places of their ritual category, and arranged instead the way they are now, it became clear that these poems of lamentation and celebration traced not only the lives of the people to whom they were dedicated, but my own life as well. This is also the reason why each poem records the date and place of composition: it mattered to me where I was when I heard the news of someone's passing; it mattered where I was when I shared someone's birthday or wedding. And in recording those dates and towns, I found I was tracing the nature of my own life, my own journeys, of exiles and returns; being away from home, travelling to other places and returning home.

Placing the poems was not always as simple as it may seem; as, for example, in the case of the poem for Alero Olympio ('Tectonics'), which was written several months after her death. The news of her passing came to me late. Should I put that poem where it would be if I were marking simply the date of her death? Or should it be placed according to when I wrote it, since that was my first ritual acknowledgement of that passing? In many instances it did not matter, because there was rarely enough time for another memorial event between the two. But in that instance there had been another sudden and tragic death, that of a child, which intervened between Alero's passing and my own inability to commemorate a lost friend.

Another concern, therefore, which became increasingly important to me as well as to my Publisher, was the need to acknowledge who these people were. Some of them are well-known public people, such as Audre Lorde, Joseph Brodsky and Nelson Mandela; yet whether they were internationally renowned or simply private people leading their own lives, I am bound to them, I knew them and many of them were my friends. All the people to whom the poems in this volume are dedicated, I knew or had the honour of meeting, with the exceptions of John Lennon and Ralph Bunche. So this is a record of my life in that sense as well. I had tea with Joseph Brodsky in his home because my mother knew his wife; I had the privilege of meeting Julius Nyerere at a ceremony in New York at which he was honoured and I met him there and again in Ghana; I met Audre Lorde on several occasions, and after the first time we met she wrote to me and encouraged and inspired me to continue writing.

Scattered amongst these public figures are my everyday friends: people such as Amy Ling and Lynne Kellerman, with whom I worked for years at Rutgers University; friends like Ariana Windle, whom I met on the streets of the little English village in which I grew up; and, of course, my family members to whom I am tied by blood and circumstance. For the most part, I remember the occasion of all these poems: that is, I remember not only the incidents and people I commemorate, but I remember actually writing them down, with the single exception of the poem for John Lennon. I had absolutely no recollection of writing that poem, until I found it again

amongst my poetry notebooks when preparing this manu-
script, while I was actually looking for the early version of the
poem "First Sonnet for Last Rites" which opens this collection,
the poem for my dead brother. (Having written those words, a
query from my editor makes me trip over one of those stum-
bling blocks of cultural translation: he was the first-born son of
my father's brother, and thus my brother- I am unable to call
him and my "cousin" first or otherwise, all our lives we have
referred to him as "Bra' Kwesi"). I knew I had that poem and
where I had kept it, and that it would need revision – and I
wanted it in the volume. Looking amongst my notebooks from
thirty years ago, I found the poem for John Lennon which will
be published almost exactly as I wrote it, twenty-five years ago.
As soon as I saw it, I recalled the writing of it: sitting on my
small trundle bed in a tiny apartment in New Haven,
Connecticut, minutes after hearing the news of his assassina-
tion; that is the only poem I have ever forgotten having drafted.

Finally, I should highlight the brief biographies at the end of
the Collection. For some of these people, there will be name
recognition but it is important to include an explanation of my
connection to them; and in the case of others, important as
they are to me, their names will not be recognisable. I have,
therefore, in addition to listing the date and place of publica-
tion beneath each poem, and the dedication above each poem,
given a brief description of each of the people for whom I have
written poems, and how they are forever connected to me.

References

Bowles, Brett C. and Hale, Thomas A. (1996) "Piloting Through
Turbulence: Grióts, Islam, and the French Encounter in Four Epics
about Nineteenth Century West African Heroes" in Kenneth
Harrow (ed), *The Marabout and the Muse: New Approaches to Islam in
African Literature* (Portsmouth NH and London: Heinemann and
James Currey), pp77-91.

Newell, Stephanie. (2006) *West African Literatures: Ways of Reading,*
(Oxford and New York: Oxford University Press), pp 124-135.

1. First Sonnet for Last Rites, for Bra' Kwesi

(For Kwesi Boaten Busia, 20 January 1946–15 May 1974)

I remember your young round face as we saw you last,
Your haunting voice sharing thoughts of eternal rest.
Busy planning a party, we took your words in jest,
And besides, how can we, so young, imagine life ending, so
    fast?
You didn't make the gathering, so I sent you some cake,
which you relished, then admonished that I'd sent no letter;
Believing we had long lifetimes to learn to do better,
We were suddenly faced with planning your wake.

You know, in truth, what makes me weep,
Are the lost occasions for such gestures of care,
A time to grow, a grief to keep;
That Easter was all the left time we had to share.
Dear brother, we did not know when we last saw you
That that would be the very last we ever saw of you.

Brandeis University, February 1975.
Accra, May 2006.

2. Flowers for Max Yergan

(19 July 1894 – 12 April 1975)

It was our last act of love;
those of us who could be there,
were as many as the red carnations
we threw in over the iron cask
in which they buried you.

Mirroring death,
the eyes of your grandchildren reflect grief
and silent horror as your coffin,
your name on it engraved with love,
was closed over your mask-like face
then swallowed up like suffocation
and lowered precisely into the earth
in the impersonal choking iron safe
built for convenience to seal in the dead
with a clang.

Breathless we buried you,
dooming fragile stems to an impassive cask,
we each threw in our helpless red carnations;
one from every one of us there,
Alone together, an act of love.

Christ Chapel, Riverside Church NYC, 16 April 1975.
Accra Ghana, March 2006.

2

3. Silver Wedding

(For My Parents: married, Wesley Memorial Church, Oxford,
14 August 1950)

After celebration
come the private moments when the guests have gone,
so this morning, early
you sneak downstairs
to tackle the abandoned dishes on the deserted table
where yesterday we gathered.
Yesterday was special:
even breakfast in bed which you dislike,
but we wished it so you obeyed;
even watching us do what you have spent the years
perfecting
while you sat idle
because we insisted
you both relax.
And so you sat
counting the days,
counting the years,
counting the children and that helped;
counting our years you realise, in one sense
it has been so short a time.

In the kitchen remember how
both laughing you rejoined us
to recall funny stories,
unable to say you could not reminisce in private
because it is all, far from over.
But we know,
you have taken the better with the bad
and still show us – only the laughter.

Opening the curtains you'll see again
the dining-room spread with flowers
and gifts from absent friends.
You were both surprised by some who remembered,
and excused those who knew
and who forgot.

The half-filled glasses of leftover wine
are all that's left of the celebration dinner
we laboured all day to bring you
on your fragile wedding china.
Facing each other across burnt-out candles
will you recall the tears
and silently treasure the toasted cheers for more
tomorrows
which begin today
with the clearing up of yesterday's feast:
celebrations leave their marks,
there are new stains on the old lace tablecloth.

Toronto, 14 August 1975.

4. The General

(For 'Katakyie' Akwasi Amankwa Afrifa,
on first seeing him after his escape from Ghana)

He had just planned
a failed revolution;
spent three weeks
crawling through forests,
watching armoured trucks
blundering to find him
as he slipped away;
when we found him,
kneeling on the nursery floor,
troubled about his children,
fitting together
pieces of a jigsaw
without a trace of fear.

Canterbury, England & Paris, France, Spring 1978.

5. Testimonies for Father

(11 July 1913–28 August 1978)

i.
Faced
with the sudden and dumbfounding call
of eternal silence
to make recompense
                              is to reach
across eternal spaces

and always and only love survives

ii.
we can not
comprehend
why every day
we feel
bereaved
anew

iii.
Time
they said
would prove the healer
Time
they said
would dull the pain

perpetual fictions

days do not dull the memories.

iv.

And if history grant us one request
we would ask
an apology
for you

v.

good memories come back now
old photographs take on new meaning
and Pa at Geneva airport
or Pa at the wedding
become Pa some twenty years before
and Pa's last picture –
random moments frozen
like fossils in an arbitrary space

vi.

Each day we find one thing
we did not ask
Each day we meet someone
we cannot share
Make some mistake
we have to solve alone
Do some great deed we can not tell.

vii.

Shared stories spill from our lips
like drops of communion wine
Time finds us still your children
and we make fellowship
with fractured pieces of life passed
like the fragments of the wafer
so many pieces of one vision
repeated in remembrance.

viii.
Resurrection is a Promise
Still
This life this ritual binds the children

and only
but always
love survives.

Oxford and Yale, August 1978 – August 1981.

6. For Lennon Who Will Never Be Sixty-Four

(9 October 1940–8 December 1980)

Someone has just shredded the sacred years of my Oxford
    childhood
When exile was an uncomprehended word,
And butterflies danced in summer light
Around the bat of Nick-Next-Door
As he taught us to play cricket in the vast green
Of our back garden, between bouts of singing
Please, Please Me, tossing his hair, and, just to impress,
Mimicking John Lennon singing *She Loves You*
Yeah.

Someone has splashed blood over buttercup days,
When war meant only one more skirmish in the battle of
    cajoling Ma,
To let us just **go** to a Beatles concert, and she bemused
and unmoved by Beatlemania, conceding only
To a house littered with their Mop Top pictures,
torn from *Girls Own* Magazine:

He gave us music and wonderful memories
Enraptured in sweet fragrant meadows of dawn and dew
And there was love all around, the *yellow submarine*,
Whose Liverpudlian sailor now lies,
So far from his childhood and mine,
Spilling his blood on a New York City street
Because a vicious someone could not bear
That all he was singing, was dreams we believed…
Imagine.

New Haven CT, 8 December 1980.

7. A Prose Poem For Lynne

(For Lynne M. Kellermann, 11 August 1947–6 December 1986)

i.
Your sudden call scattered my meditations:
>kneeling on my floor surrounded by words and
>images of women holding hands, women working,
>women living, women birthing –

you tell me you
are dying.

Your voice whose strength deceived us
>because it never grew frail
>holds steady as

you tell me you
are dying.

And we shared a shattered silence

Then, urgent with a desire for living
but with nothing fine or profound to say
to consecrate the moment,
our voices speak of everything
and nothing after
you tell me you
are dying.

But, friend, what words could we have found
to save us from our terror?
What words could we have found
to protect us from the moment
or restore us to the moment
before the moment the words were spoken,
when we could still pretend a hope?

Who knows if words of certain death
separate us from miracles;
but somehow there seemed greater space for one before
human voices pronounced a
Judgement.

Am I dying?
Yes.
How long...?

Through the echo of conversation
runs through thought:
        And was our combined Faiths not sufficient
        for this one so fervently desired miracle?
        Did we mistake some formula of prayer?
                Or are miracles born, not of hope,
                but of the measure of our despair?

Is not the Lord in Zion?
The harvest is past and the summer is ended and we are not
    saved.
For the hurt of the daughter of my people I am hurt.
Is there no balm in Gilead; is there no physician there?
Why then is the health of the daughter of my people not
    recovered?[1]

ii.
How Long?
I want to hold you close and with my strength
give you the promise of continued life.
But like the astonished prophet can only hurt my rage
into the vacuum of my bewilderment

---

1. Jeremiah 8:19-22.

Looking for reassurance and solace I return
to fragments of paper on the floor
to recollect images of living
but they are gone, replaced
by visions of women in mourning:
>
>   my mother's hands in a gesture of love
>   and prayer
>   closing father's eyes at his moment of dying –
>   the hands of his sister preparing his exiled body
>   for the final journey home:

my fractured meditations have been altered by your voice
reminding me
of the relentlessness of dying.

I want to hold you close with my strength
give you the promise of continued living.
And can only write these words for you
out of an early sorrow.

iii.
Yet is the journey over?
We have a promise of more than this.
And for what place have you left us, you
who were always so good to say where
you were headed, or at least
why?

We remain in Gilead:
>
>   to secure an inheritance for those they loved best
>   the warriors crossed over Jordan first,
>   the beloved in crossing remind the living
>   of the balm we inherit by Grace.

And you, finally, in peace have gone before
so it is we who must now be still and know
the road through living is not just wilderness,
and the place we part company is not a desolation
but the last meeting point on our different journeys.

So Leah, daughter of Jerusalem,
we sat shiva[2] for you
and we were glad you walked this way for a while.

Leah, daughter of Jerusalem,
we sing songs for you
For we are glad we walked together, awhile.

Bryn Mawr and Rutgers, December 1986.

---

2. My friend Lynne was Jewish; 'shiva' is the Hebrew word for the customary
   seven day mourning period, akin to a seven day wake, or like the "sitting"
   in the home of the bereaved which takes place in different communities in
   Ghana after seven days.

8. Sermons from Riverside

(For William Sloane Coffin, on his retirement as
Senior Minister of Riverside Church)

Choices
At the moment of hesitation before the knife falls,
we are both Abraham and Isaac
trapped:

this razor's edge of human choice
is all we ever had.

'The promise of life's magnificence' is perplexing
There never was an original innocence
only this original contradiction;
This world is our embattled Eden
of eternal seconds of human decision
on the tips of our outstretched hands.

And every movement becomes a choice
and each choice a bewildering journey
with no clear signpost, save one;

To face Mount Sinai all footsteps stumble, through
the Wilderness of Sin.

And the sound of the serpent's hiss,
or the bleating of the ram in the thicket,
have never penetrated the silence of Gethsemane.
With no pre-ordained sign, we make the resolution
to stretch out the fingers, to pull back the hand;
to pull back the fingers, to lower the hand.

Through Faith
before the Promise dies, the Lamb cried
and astonished children climb off the altar.

New Brunswick and New York, April 1987.

14

9. Testament For The First Accused

(Nelson Mandela, For The Twenty-Seven Years)

I know Patrice Lumumba had been sometime dead,
    and Sylvanus Olympio only just, though I'm not sure why,
As I try to reconnect myself with my child's mind
    and the memories of events that jumble there –
A knowledge of our distant world pieced together,
    through overheard conversations, and voices on the radio.

In 1962 the world was a very different place.

I didn't know where Montgomery was,
    but learnt the meaning of boycott.
Didn't understand Mau Mau,
    except it taught the impact of lies,
    and what all freedoms cost.
I remember your name, and vague talk of a trial
    and treason being a serious thing;
Sisulu and Mbeki, Goldberg and Mhlaba,
Kathrada, Motsoaledi and Mlangeni, at Rivonia;
These names I have learnt through the years,
But at the time, what I recall for sure
Is Abebe Bikila's second Olympic gold,
And Cassius Clay proving he was the greatest,
By the time you made your statement
And disappeared.

We have not seen you since.

I didn't mark your fiftieth birthday:
But in Ghana J. B. Danquah was already dead,
And we had lived through coups and counter-coups already
At the start of a second republic.
While Baldwin warned of *The Fire Next Time*
The white Rhodesians declared UDI,
And the Zimbabweans braced for war.
But we were killing our brothers already in Biafra
While the world watched,
And a young Christopher Okigbo reminded us
That even the poets were dying.
And you were still alive,
And you were still not free.

Though James Brown danced us off the streets,
And *Soul came to Soul* in Ghana
No-one remembered Paul Robeson, and
Mahalia Jackson sung her last.
Singing *We Shall Overcome*
Through frustrated Freedom Summers we left
Mississippi, Watts and Newark burning -
And Medgar, Malcolm, and Martin dead. All dead.
And you were still alive,
And you were still not free.

In an angry and lonely world,
We marked the passage of your tenth year
Reading *Letters to Martha* and *Soledad Brother*
All *Souls were on Ice*
As Arthur Nortje killed himself in an Oxford room,
And an exiled Kabaka died.
We freed Angela Davis, but on your desolate island
You were still alive,
And you were still not free.

Your sixtieth birthday reminded us
This struggle was your life,
But by then your life had become our struggle,
As we buried Hector Petersen
And a hundred slaughtered children
On the scorched streets of Soweto.
With a jailed Thandi Modisi
We *Cried Freedom* for a murdered Stephen Biko;
People young enough to be your children,
And children younger than your children dead,
So many of them dead.
Yet you at least were still alive,
But you were still not free.

We shouted FRELIMO and another Empire fell.
Antonio Jacinto *Survived Tarrafal*,
But Agostinho Neto was dead.
Eduardo Mondlane had been many years murdered,
And we have since mourned the wreckage of Samora Machel
On the South African side of Mozambique's mountains.
But you were still alive,
And you were still not free.

By your twentieth year,
Anwar Sadat had sued for peace in the Knesset,
And had been later killed for his pains.
And Haile Selassie, the lion of Judah had disappeared,
Leaving no memorial, except a three-thousand year
Imperial kingdom, now decades at war.

And in the Eritrea, Tigre, the Sudan, the Spanish Sahara
The *Harvest of our Dreams Reaped a Whirlwind* of nightmares.
And we searched for Janani Luwum among Kampala's
    martyred.
Marley who sang for Manley and Mugabe was so young dead.
But you were still alive,
And you were still not free.

The decades bring deaths of leaders,
The power and the myth that was Nkrumah –
Lie broken, like his shattered statue
On the Accra streets.
And in the same week that Jomo Kenyatta
Faced his sacred Mount Kenya for the final time
Kofi Busia's *Challenge to an Africa in Search of Democracy*
Ended. All your peers dead.
But you were still alive,
And you were still not free.

Yet, on a continent being 'liberated', 'redeemed',
    'revolutionised',
Proclaiming *Uhuru*, the people were marching:
Twenty-five years after Sharpeville, we march,
Ten years after Soweto, we march,
And when they killed mothers and babies
On their march through Mamelodi,
Still, with them, we march.
For you were still alive,
And you were still not free.

By the time we reached your seventieth birthday,
Another generation of children
Had learned to call your name.
We carry old images of your face in our hearts,
And on the T-shirts on our backs,
As an icon of a new morning.
The Tembu warrior prince, the lawyer-activist,
The prisoner.
Around the world we marched in our millions,
Demanding your return, into a troubled world
So sadly bereft of heroes.
For you were still alive,
And you were still not free.

You disappeared from our view
From a world which had taken: no small step on the moon
    for man;
No Apollos, no Challengers, no Salyuts,
No photographs of the furthest planets, no walks in space.
The small steps taken on earth for mankind had included:
No Flower Power Love concerts at Woodstock,
No-One Love Peace concerts in Kingston, Jamaica,
No Art Against Apartheid Freedom concerts in Sun City,
No Bands in Aid Proclaiming *We Are The World*.
That world had known: no 'Cultural Revolution' in China,
No drafted US troops in Vietnam,
No 'Killing Fields' in Cambodia,
No vanished *Prisoner Without a Name*
in a *Cell Without a Number*, mourned by the
Mothers of the Plaza de Mayo; And through all this
You were still alive,
And you were still not free.

And now, it is the Lord's Day, the eleventh of February 1990,
And it is five a.m. in Los Angeles, California,
It is eight a.m. in New York and Kingston, Jamaica,
It is one p.m. in Stockholm, London and Accra, Ghana,
And half the marching world has paused -
To keep vigil;
For it is three p.m. in Cape Town, South Africa,
And we wait to see your face.

After twenty-seven years of fighting, marching, and singing
We keep a ninety-minute watch;
To see you take these next few steps
On this your *No Easy Walk*
To our uncertain *Freedom*;
To witness your release into this changing world,
Unceasingly the same.
For you are still alive,
But we are still not free.
Amandla, Mandela
A Luta Continua!

Los Angeles CA, 11 February 1990.

10. For Anyone of You Who Knows I Am Your Sister

(For Audre Lorde)

I know the story of a man, who happened to be Catholic,
behaved like a Good Samaritan and saved a brother from
   drowning.
At least, he tried.
And the drowning was literal, not metaphorical.
But by the ocean's edge he realised,
there being only so much beating a body can bear,
he needed to offer another salvation
and he asked for rites for the dying.

This prayer became controversy.
What if the dying man were Muslim?
What if, even if another Christian, he wasn't a Catholic at all?
What if he had some other Faith? What if... What if...?
And amidst all this speculation and burning anger
No-one seemed to reach out and celebrate
this one simple fact:
He had acted out of love.

Death is our final necessity.
But alive we resist it with every living breath,
until in the face of defeat, and grievings out of season,
we reach out with passion with what we know
and give ourselves in rituals.
Not necessarily what is needed, but with what we have
   inside us,
when that is all there is left to give.

There is always anger at the losings,
and a generation of our brothers is dying
on the concrete battlefields of city streets,
the suddenness of their deaths unmarked
by any rituals of departure.
Death they are called a 'lost generation',
Yet not in concession to that naming, but as a battle-cry.
Not in acceptance of that horror,
but in a calling out the greater crime
that permits their murder
and coldly counts the dead.

There are so many discrepancies of gesture.
We none of us know each other's language
or learn identical rituals.

Yet can we living embrace transgressive actions
which flout all conventions, even our own,
that have their source in love?
For in the end, we are all beaten by the wayside,
bleeding broken on city streets,
or drowning.
And in the end, in the end,
I'll reach for the hand of anyone
who even cares I'm dying.

'I Am Your Sister' Conference
Boston MA, 6 October 1990.

11. A Lamentation for Audre Lorde

(18 February 1934–7 November 1992)

Damrifa, Damrifa, Damrifa Due, Due, Due,
Yebo afena kye wo Safohene, Safohene, Safohene.

Sister Outsider, whose name has many other spellings – hear
us;

> This is a song from sorrowing soldiers, as we lay our
> sister to rest;
> A song of suffering sisters, as we lay our soldier to rest.
> *Damarifa, Damrifa Due*:

You who taught us, To stand eye to eye, Measure our fears,
Channel our angers:

> In this world of wailing women, now we lay our warrior
> to rest,
> With these words of warriors weeping, as we lay our
> woman to rest. *Damarifa, Damrifa Due*:

You who taught us: Dismantle Master's house, Liberate his
wives, Empower his slaves:

> This is a song from sorrowing soldiers, as we lay our
> sister to rest;
> A song of suffering sisters, as we lay our soldier to rest.
> *Damarifa, Damrifa Due*:

You who taught us: Celebrate our difference, Affirm our
  wellness, Unleash our erotic:

  Into this world of wailing women; now we lay our
    warrior to rest,
  With these words or warriors weeping, oh we lay our
    woman to rest. *Damarifa, Damrifa Due*

You who poured love in us: To transform our silences, Claim
  our languages, And Act:

  This is a song from sorrowing soldiers, as we lay our
    sister to rest;
  A song of suffering sisters, as we lay our soldier to rest.
    Damarifa, Damrifa Due:

Damrifa, Damrifa, Damrifa Due, Due, Due,
Yebo afena kye wo Safohene, Safohene, Safohene.

Memorial Service, Rutgers University, November 1992.

Akan Proverb: *Akofena Kunim ko a, wobo afena kye no safohene* – Meaning a retir-
ing great warrior deserves a royal sword of rest.
Damrifa Due: An expression of sorrow and condolence, but addressed to the
deceased, not the living.

12. A Wedding Song

(For Chic Streetman and Karen Sorenson on their Wedding Day)

This is your first song together.

As with certain voices you claim
a sudden love
making peace with solitary pasts
to walk together
into the mystery of a future
forever bound

Remember – a future forever bound
is a rugged path forever blessed;
for marriage is the first rite
of miracles of human faith,
its vows our unique and sacred songs

And to be surprised by love
is to be caressed
by the sudden touch of God.

New York, NY, 2 October 1993.

13. Addresses: 93 Abingdon Road, 1963–93

(For Mama, on her Seventieth Birthday)

The road home has always passed through
the crossroads by the 'Hinds Head' at Kingston Bagpuize,
Where the A420 snakes across the A415; our Abingdon Road.
Turn right at the Apple Farm and go straight for three miles.

At the first mile, look west at the top of the hill, before the
   sharp descent.
From late autumn when the trees are bare
the low hills of the Windrush Valley huddle towards you in
   the distance.

At the second mile, where the Windrush finally meets the
   Thames,
Summer brings competing crowds to either side of the old
   Roman Bridge.
In the 'Maybush' locals, anglers and farmers fiercely
guard their privacy against the outside visitors, holiday
   makers, society diners,
and boating Thames travellers revelling at the Rose Revived.

The third mile begins with the Standlake garage; the
same family – Alfred, Roger, Peter, and now Pauline –
have owned it all these years.
It ends with the historic 'Golden Balls', a pub under
the sign of the pawnbroker. That changed hands once too
   often
and now stands boarded up, abandoned.
But if you reach there, turn back.
You have passed our house by half-a-mile.

It looked like all the others except
the quiet wildness of the garden mother planted... all alone,
her mid-wife hands first birthed babies,
then nursed seedlings, tamed shrubberies, and planted
every single living tree
on this patch of earth to which we are entitled,
and except for the name on the wrought iron gate which
    marks our difference;
Da/dwen – to sleep and ponder-,
which we have done in this place of sojourn
for thirty years now.

We arrived in mid-December winter,
in time to greet the heaviest snowfall of the century.
Four-foot high snow drifts dwarfed us
as we played our way to school
in the only winter weather of my life
I recollect as fun.

And so it is that wherever in the world I am,
I return by this road to this ancient village full of children
And this ageing house, shrouded by still blossoming things
In anticipation of the refuge of one warm,
One more wondrous
One more Windrush Valley Spring.

Accra, 5 April 1994.

Dadwen means to sleep and ponder in the Akan language in Ghana.

14. Secrets and Gifts

(For Nana Dokua Akufo-Addo At Ten)

Prologue
The last time I saw you, you were sleeping.
I walked into the room to give you a kiss, my goodbye
     gift.
You whimpered, raised your arms as if to hug me
and rolled over, still asleep.
You didn't hear me enter, you didn't hear me leave the
     room.

i. Airports
Earlier that summer, at Gatwick, we went last-minute
     shopping,
choosing gifts for friends and relations,
amidst a plethora of Swatch watches, perfumes and clothes
you made a secret confession:
          "I'm buying a present for my friend",
a boy whose picture you keep in your schoolbook,
          "so please don't tell daddy."
As if he wouldn't guess
who a five-pound slab of chocolate was for.

Eight hours too late,
we played clapping games at Lagos,
to pass away the time.
In Dutch, I taught you the only pat-a-cake game I remember,
a gift from my drifting childhood that haunts my days
          "papagaai leef je noch
          eyee aa deyee aa,
          ja meneer, ich ..."
Your games were more rooted, rhythmic and complicated –
at two o'clock in the morning I kept missing the beat
and mixing up my hands.

"I'll teach that baby boy," you said,
as you left me, hands skip-stopped in mid-air,
missing your touch.

But your declaration at Kotoka was the real surprise.
            "Oh that Auntie of mine doesn't like you at all',
as you proceeded to tell me the litany of outrages
she had accused me of all summer long;
            "but don't tell *anyone* I told you,
            or I'm in *deep* trouble,"
as we burst out in shared laughter at the secret.
In a whip-lash season of raw betrayals
you gifted loyalty as a balm,
so no, I won't tell a soul.

ii. Funfairs and Other Amusements
You have had enough of trouble,
woman-child in a world turned tragically grown up.
With a wisdom that surprises
you, assert a happiness; for yourself,
and those, like me, your life caresses.

So you took me driving at the arcades.
I called them dodgems, you called them bumper cars,
and showed the difference that drives you onwards.
            "But Auntie Abena, you too must have fun today",
so off we went, I in mini-skirt and stockinged feet,
you in my high-heeled shoes;
you taught me ten-pin bowling
and showed me how you beat the odds.

You gave me only two commands:
that whenever I showed up, I was to teach you
first to fry Old English sausages
the way your daddy liked them,
and then, to make jellies.

So we went shopping for foods, exotic and banal,
Indian spices and Cornflakes,
Cadbury's Roses and Smoked Scotch Salmon,
and frying chicken by the bucket.
But selecting the sausages took the most time.
          "Nice child your daughter," offered the cabby
as we hauled our load into his car.
You hugged me as you climbed in beside me,
and simply smiled.
That was your other gift;
for one short five minute drive, I could pretend;
for one brief moment I could *not* concede
to an already knowing world
that you weren't in fact, *my* daughter.

Epilogue
When last I saw your mother alive, you were sleeping;
I walked into the room and gave her a hug, a surprise
          hello.
You were two years old and whimpering,
restive in your sleep.
"Can I hold her?" I asked overjoyed to see you,
so grown, so changed since your birth.

Walking up and down, we laughed together
till you stayed asleep in my arms.
Before I left, she showed me where to lay you down;
you rolled over, still asleep.
You didn't hear me enter, you didn't hear me leave the room,
Though she lifted you and handed you to me,
like a secret gift;
a sacred trust.

                                        Accra, 21 May 1995.

15. Let's Light Another Candle

(For the fourteen Montreal Martrys,
and the fourteen × fourteen million women more)

...Let's light a candle

Let's light another candle
For old women, rejected wives, and all women
        powerless and silenced,
whose children have forgotten the ones who gave them birth
Let's light a candle,

Let's light another candle,
For childless wives, violated women and all women scorned
whose brothers have forgotten the same mothers they
    mourned
Let's light a candle,

Let's light another candle
For women mutilated by parents, battered by partners,
        all women killed by laws of custom,
whose families hold sacrosanct such 'cultural practice',
Let's light a candle,

Let's light another candle
For 'comfort women', 'ethnically polluted' women,
        all women brutalised by rape and the sanctions of war
whose states have abandoned them; displaced, seeking refuge
Let's light a candle,

Let's light another candle
For girl children unmourned in death, oppressed in life,
    all girls unborn to life,
whose people place no honour in girls
Let's light a candle,

Let's light another candle
Also for warrior women working for women,
all females, all feminists, all sisters in spirit,
Let's light a candle,

Let's light another candle…

Accra, 6 December 1995.

16. The Voice of Joseph Brodsky: In Memoriam

(24 May 1940–28 January 1996)

Into our stillness
Your voice sounded forth,
In-can-ta-tion:
Unorthodox Cantor of the Russian steppes,
Your magnetic words
Proclaimed your travails
And pulled on ours to meet you
In communion.

Courage has its own invisible signposts;
So your wandering footsteps guided
Us, pilgrims on uncharted pathways –
Surprised us onwards;
Your impassioned words
Encircled
Our expectations: a clarion call
Ennobling us to journey on, knowing
The gladness of every grace note
of conviction.

New Brunswick, NJ, 30 January 1996.

17. Of Memory and Loss

(For Pa: On The Dedication Of His Tomb On The Twentieth Anniversary Of His Passing)

Beneath God's tree we have kept vigil for two decades:
Injustice leaves turmoil in its wake,
And we still struggle against its tides.

We grow battle weary.

We tell ourselves the dead miss their tombstones
Like sleepers miss the pillows on their beds.
This is not true.

We miss the monuments
As the foundations of our memories crack with time,
And we cling to different fragments of truth.

What is the meaning of death in the face of time?

What lingers always is the memory of loss:
Memorials are the foundations we prepare
To defy the tricks of time.

Elegies are lullabies to rock the already sleeping dead,
Subterfuges for the living; like parents clinging to a child
And singing, long after the infant has been lulled to sleep.

What is the meaning of time in the face of death?

I cling to an anger that will not yield to this truth –
I miss the sound of your laughter, and the touch of your
hand.
It is that simple.

Slowly, like falling silk cotton in the wind,
We have found the resolution of a truce:

This should have been a happy song,
But I can't sing in tune,
And I can't sing through tears.

This effort is as hard as the granite we have etched,
Lovingly but war worn, to fulfill our half-kept promise.
We ask your forgiveness.

Slowly, like falling silk cotton in the winds of time,
We have come to revelations:

Beneath God's tree we have kept vigil for two decades:
And the sleep of the Just makes no earthly sound,
So your spirit is quiet:

Because the meaning of death, and the meaning of time,
like the meaning of life, is God's Love.

Wenchi, Brong Ahafo – Ghana, 28 August 1998.

18. Venetian Glass

(Amy Ling, 9 May 1939–21 August 1999; In Loving Memory)

One thirtieth birthday belt
Well-worn and frayed,
One book of poems, signed -
A pair of wing frame chairs
borrowed for twenty years
and never returned,
Plus several random snap shots
more precious than I knew.

Already we collect the left pieces
of your precious life, like trophies;
Those are mine.

That steelness of spirit that made you endure
Will ensure the memories last:
And the laughter remains, and the love.

For my Anglo-Ghanaian wedding, you
my China-American friend, gave me
Venetian Glass.
In all shades of blue
our many worlds reflect,
assayed and true.

One thirtieth birthday belt,
One book of poems
A pair of wing frame chairs,
Random snap shots,
And Venetian Glass.
Your last gift, our last encounter;
Venetian Glass;
Cobalt as your dress, royal
sapphire, aquamarine, azure -
In all shades of blue
our many worlds connect,
assayed and true.

Rutgers University, October 1999.

19. *Mwalimu:* Teacher

(For President Julius Nyerere, March 1922–14 October 1999)

Mwalimu means teacher,
and at your calling home,
that was the only name
we knew you by.

Mwalimu,
for your legacy of Faith,
we embrace you:
Uhuru na Ujamaa
For your principles of Freedom,
we applaud you.
For the Justice of your ideals,
we honour you.
For the courage of your faltered plans,
we salute you.

Mwalimu, teacher,
yours was a goodness that is great.
For the simple dignity of your tasks,
we commend you
to the Lord
who grants his tireless servants
the bounty of eternal rest.

African Studies Association Conference,
Philadelphia, PA, November 1999.

20. The Healer's Heart

*(For My Brother-in-Law, Dr Louis Kofi Essandoh,
on the occasion of his being honoured by the American Heart
Association of Anne Arundel County MD)*

What matters to you is the heart,
In all its actual power,
In all its inspired meanings.
In actual fact,
We each have one, and only one,
That pumps, until it comes to rest
In its own indeterminable time:
The driving force of being.

Yet your instrument is that one heart,
And you, trained mechanic of its mysteries,
Know how to keep it whole,
With knowledge, with skill,
And with the sacred fire of hope;
For the heart inspires, the heart records
The pain and promise of our lives:
The essential source of being.

And this at least we know,
Husband, father, doctor, friend,
And brother -
All hearts pump blood,
But not all hearts are good, and brave, and kind;
And in you, physician of the compassionate art,
The doctor's hand and the engineer's mind
Are guided by a noble healer's heart.

                                    Annapolis, MD, 28 April 2001.

21. And What Remains

(For Mrs Christine Afrifa, on the occasion of twenty-three years
after his assassination on June 26 1979, of the Final Funeral Rites
for her Late Husband 'Katakyie' Akwasi Amankwa Afrifa)

and what remains?
a woman over twenty years his widow, after barely ten
    years his bride;
a lifetime keeping wake, our dead hero's spirit, restless, by
    her side.

and what remains?
for some of us, the magic heroes of our youth never die;
sometimes they grow up into other selves we do not
    understand,
sometimes they die too young to change,
living in our hearts forever grand,

sometimes, something in between

as, like his orphaned children, we must learn
that to be the hero of one story is to be prepared
to be the villain of another, told by your adversary:
this man was prepared.

the magic almost worked;
the bullets couldn't make him die, at least, not easy, and
    not soon:
such contradictions of torment and triumph
of a life well meant.

and what remains?
to lay to final rest the bones of a man, of soaring restless
    fervour,
and inextinguishable valour.

26 January 2002.

22. Warrior, Father, Nobleman

(Baafuor Osei Akoto: 22 February 1904–3 September 2002;
In Grateful Memory)

Warrior, Father, Nobleman:
Let us now own the lives loved, the battles lost,
the loves lost, the victories won,
and the people you became.

Fighter on a mission, carrying your word
from the palace to castle, from castle to prison cell and back,
and back again; exiled linguist of the rejected staff,
returned to kiss the Great Sword of your nation and elevate
    your stool.

There are so many legacies –
so many kings served and queens buried,
offspring named and sacred mysteries upheld.

Not all lives are legends, but yours was so many
the regrets can be only ours,
that there will be no more stories.

That tongue which was your sword,
which roused rebels to a cause
and dispensed the alluvial wisdom of the proverbs
to those who understood,

Is now still.

That grave voice of gravel
that told as many stories
as it kept secrets,
has held its last counsel.

Walk home well, brave spirit.
As your last post sounds,
retiring great warrior, we award you
your royal sword of rest, to say

This was a warrior, this a chief, this a man and father.

So we mourn, but will not taunt the gods by grieving
a long life so richly blessing,
and so blessed.

Kumasi – Ghana, 13 November 2002.

23. A Poem on Transitions

(For Mama on my Fiftieth Birthday, Monday, 28 April 2003)

I, a worshipper, am a Tuesday born.

I know amongst your people on the Atlantic Coast
Tuesdays are sacred to the oceans
Whose undertows and tides direct the lives
Of those who work on them
Or, like us, who cross them.

And on this sacred Sunday past
I waited until just past midnight
To call you in Accra
For the first voice I heard on this day
to be yours.

Had I been in my place on the Jersey shore
I would have been facing the correct ocean of history
To send my prayers across in salutation.

Yet now, early on this Monday that marks
My half-century in transit on this earth,
A life marked by oceans and the borders
We have crossed, you and I,
Here at this resort on Pacific waters
Facing shark-surrounded Catalina Island
I am facing records of other histories
and other ancient gods.

Now, where you are,
As it would have been on the day of my birth,
In the unchanging nature of tropical seasons
It is a little more than half an hour before sunset.
5:50 p.m. on Greenwich Mean in April
is 10:50 a.m. on the West Coast of North America,
where I am thinking of you in this hour of slow transitions,

As I run and walk this beach with my sister.
She has brought me here
To honour that rite of passage of separation
From you so long ago, of me,
Your third child and first-born daughter
of raucous laughter,
Your Tuesday born, your child of fire.

In your neat, meticulous hand
You marked my arrival on this day
in the old Gold Coast diary
your long-dead father preserved;
"Delivered 5:50pm. 5lbs 11ozs, a girl".
There is almost nothing else noted the entire year,
Except at the back, a list of things to do,
And the cost of bread and eggs.

When they cooked palm-oiled yam and boiled eggs for us
Did they also sprinkle yam and shark meat on the seas?
Or are we free to let all old gods starve
Because the Lamb of God no longer demands sacrifices of
Pigeons, or goats, or all those slaughtered cows?

The moment of my birth
Finds me on my knees in quiet meditation,
facing eastwards to other far horizons;
turning across the continent towards that other ocean
that binds me to you on its further shore.
To offer up for you my quiet prayer
From a heart which your love has made large
From the blessing name you gifted me
Adompim – that I may love thousands.

In honour of my father, now passed away
a whole half of my life
And in praise to you, my living mother,
I raise up my hands to the long risen sun
Now reaching near its potential in the late morning light.

I pray our new ancient prayer of Benediction
That the Lord Bless you and keep you
And lift up his countenance upon you,
That The Lord may shine upon you, and give you peace.

For the grace you show your children
in our joys and errant ways,
For the honour you show friends,
Through the pain of all your days;

For the love of the man you married,
And your loyalty to his name;
For your steadfastness in trials
Of the statesmen he became.

Note: *Adompim* means "one who loves thousands", and again – in the Akan language of Ghana.

For your wisdom, and your patience,
In the paths you've walked alone,
Know our blessedness is knowing
Where you are, and Faith is home.

Los Angeles CA, New Brunswick NJ and Accra,
Ghana, April 2003 – April 2008.

24. A Posthumous Letter to Lemuel Johnson

(On the Second Anniversary of His Passing)

The Bell Tower Hotel
Ann Arbor, Michigan
Saturday, 13 March 2004.

Dear Lemuel,

I don't remember when last I wrote to you, but it's been years, not to say decades. We didn't write, we were not intimate enough, nor far enough apart for that. Only lovers and separated relatives write these days, (and most lovers are forgetting how). We spoke when we met, and then, like all late-twentieth century people, within these shores at least, we became first telephone and then email people.

The more's the pity.

But then, that's perhaps an appropriate way to begin; on the distance between pen and ink and digital messages and what they mean. We are here to honour you, our teacher, mentor and friend. That, unfortunately, in the way we live our lives, means you have passed away, and we want to make sure you do not become confined only to that past, a thing of the past. And we are also here to think about our present and our future, so in your honour we try to articulate what it is about you we carry with us into that uncertain future.

Of course the future is always uncertain, for everyone; the difference is between those of us who must live our lives always cognisant of that uncertainty, and those of us who bestride the worlds we inhabit, large or small, like colossi; as if the only future we have to contend with is the one of our own making, that we can stamp out with our seven-league hobnail boots and wrest with our own hands. We have one or two of them roaming about these days, but unlike the Emperors of old, they are not building libraries, and there's one or two things they don't know; never even knew in order to forget. From Port au Prince to Baghdad, you know who's, or is it you know what's, still rush in where angels have always feared to tread. 'The hand that made us is Divine': what a wonderful hymn; but some forget that that does not mean we too have divine hands, and if we think that, what we touch, destroys. So most of us live in a world where the uncertainties, not of life in the abstract, but living in the concrete, dog our literal heels.

That is one of the things you showed us, how we came to be this way; and in verse, no less.

We are still struggling for the world to hear you, Lemuel, to hear *us*.

Yesterday on my way here, I showed *Highlife for Caliban* to the stranger sitting beside me on the seats at the gate at Newark airport, waiting two hours for the delayed plane that brought us here. I wanted her to read your introduction 'How To Breathe Dead Hippo Meat and Live'; she read some of the poems too. What she said was interesting: "Who is his audience? I'm Jewish, so I understand the Biblical references, but what about all the others? If I can see the richness of the allusions I'm getting, what about the ones I'm missing?" I tried to explain, that that was your point. At least *she* understood, and so we try, one person at a time.

We, Diaspora Africans, whilst making our own history, also became the inheritors of so many histories we are said to have fallen outside of, with which we can fashion the world anew. We are sacred wordsmiths, always have been. But what is the value of our esoteric knowledge? Is knowledge power only when everyone knows you have it? Does that explain how the ignorant, equipped with armies, can become so powerful? And always it is our labour which makes them so.

A few years ago, maybe ten years now, I went to visit Ayi Kwei Armah, and we walked along the beach at Popenguine in Senegal. I looked around me and teased him, thinking of what it looked like in the villages outside Takoradi where he is from. "You think you've come to a new place," I said, "but you haven't; you're still living in a place that looks like the shores on which you were born." He laughed. Only, the sand on the beach was black, and shiny. "A by-product of the computer age," he said, 'they need something from it to make the computers work." "And the leftovers are cubic zirconias," I offered. "Exactly," he said. Isn't this a familiar story, Sethe worrying that she made the ink; what they write with may have changed, but how they are equipped to write, has not.

I too own a computer, so I should not say 'they', I should say 'we'. That is one of the worries: we have become sojourners here in Babylon Redux, and I, at least, worry about the fact that there are more computers on one campus at Rutgers than there are in all the ministries in Accra. What does this still mean? What weapons can we forge in this war, when the blood on our city streets is often our own, spilled by our own brothers. Have we made Freetown free?

We continue to try.

Our poverty has never been of the mind, nor always of the spirit. But it is true, those have always been hard to hold on to when the flesh is weak, literally, from hunger. (There is no protection from those other metaphorical weaknesses, I guess). What battles we must continue to wage are always those against the idea of a history we have not made. Something has been haunting me: a few months ago, I was listening to a colleague give a fascinating talk about an alternative system of doing algebraic fractions, based on an ancient Egyptian method. When he broke it down, it was so logical and simple. What troubled me was that I had never even heard of this possibility; it is a way of doing mathematics that was never taught; that was bad enough, but I was unsettled to discover, once again as if this were new, that we are taught to believe that there is only one way of doing mathematics... and this other way, which is based upon the binary system that now drives computers, was discovered around the time of the pyramids.

Last month, being driven from Cairo to Alexandria, I was looking out of the window – and there they were! For five thousand years or so, anyone – anyone at all – walking that road has looked up in that direction over those same fields and seen them, standing there; 'They say man fears time, but time fears the pyramids.' How can we forget so much? How can we ignore so much?

One volume of *Women Writing Africa* is out now, another is all but finished, and the last two are in preparation. Thank you again for that faith in us that supported us from the outset. Fourteen years ago, when we started, we did not know it was going to consume two decades of our lives. Trying to put forward women's knowledge, our knowledge, and how we have shaped our history. How can we have been outside of history, his-story, when even the lullabies we sing to our children trace the minutiae of events historical. The ritual we impose when a woman dies in childbirth re-enacts the sacred story of creation; a child in Niger is lulled to sleep being reassured she is even more valuable than the salt on which their livelihood depends; young girls in Burkina lament lovers leaving for Bamako; and wives are wary of the beauty of Kumasi.

We have sung about it all, and written it too: in 1739 a slave woman born in Poppo, living in St Thomas, petitions the Queen of Denmark about the conditions under which they live and worship; in 1838 a former slave, born in North Carolina and newly arrived in Freetown, petitions her late master's lawyer concerning the resettlement funds promised at manumission, and still not received; and in 1934, a widow in Casamance petitions the authorities for the value of the cows from her late husband's estate, which his relatives are not handing over; same letter, different age. Yet the attempt is always made, with the same courage to each new naked emperor, and whatever people think, our actions survive.

We are on the same old coast, Lemuel, the carnival has not stopped, but we still know all the dances, old and new. What a joy it was to dance with you! Continue the Highlife in Heaven for us. We still hear you, and step with you.

Much Love,

25. Busia Family Tribute for Mrs Adeline Akufo-Addo

(17 December 1917–21 March 2004)

Adeline Sylvia Eugenia Ama Yeboakua: let us begin with how well your fathers named you. Your names were chosen well, and given well. The princess of their hearts, in the glory of the Akim woods they named you noble, and well born. Their auspicious voices proclaimed you the hope of all your royal clans of blood and of spirit.

And what clans they were which claimed you; Ofori-Atta, Danquah, Akufo-Addo. As daughter, niece, sister, wife and mother you carry the names of so many from our history. Your mothers taught you well, service and hospitality are royal duties; palaces give no shelter from the invisible work of being a woman. Once learned, this you never forgot. To enter your home was to be hosted and made welcome. But all this is part of the public record. Your passing brings for us, as well, a host of private memories.

To a generation of us you were first simply yourself – Adeline Ofori-Atta. In the late 1930s Naa-Morkor Bruce (later Busia) remembers the most popular senior girl at Achimota; a striking beauty, vivacious, athletic and private, who paid surprising kind attention to her, a little girl, newly arrived in school, the youngest of her peers. She remembers when you broke your leg that would not heal, the pain it caused and how it changed your life. She remembers also, years later – a pupil midwife too junior to attend to such a momentous event – the excitement in Korle-Bu Teaching hospital the day you delivered lawyer Akufo-Addo's first-born son.

To another generation of us, the generation of Naa-Morkor's children, you were the matriarch of the most dazzling family of our peers. We remember discovering them on our return home from England in the late 1960s, and how we saw them then – eloquent and French-speaking, with style and charm. They were witty, bright, and clever.

To yet another generation, the Busia children's children, you were the grandmother, sighted at church services or the occasional family party. Visiting you was a wonder to their young eyes. Surrounded by mementos of a momentous life, even your bed, piled high with old newspapers, photographs, and letters you were sorting through, was a history lesson.

And that is why we write today. To bear witness to that history and the journey we have shared. We join the honour guard of those who wish you well and add our voices to the chorus of the praise song for your life. Let us then close with our last verse to your fidelity; your loyalty to our late father, Kofi Abrefa Busia of Wenchi, and to the cause. In the days of struggle, you and yours were there. In the days of joy, you and yours were there. In the days of darkness, you were there. We have fought together, laughed together, mourned together, and for this we mourn you now.

They say that on that last Sunday you were here with us on earth, your broken leg, which got better but never got well, was finally healed, for which you declared you were going to go to give thanks to God. As you dance your way to the final church service of eternal life, we clap hallelujah for you. You have walked well. May you dance with joy through eternity.

Accra, 11 May 2004.

26. Ring Shout for the Ancestors

(For Sterling Stuckey on his retirement)

Sterling sets the standard
for the qualities of worth,
from the core of burnished silver
to constant acts of character,
and you exemplify how we've been tempered,
and worn well.

I've been 'buked and I've been scorned: yes,
my foot bone broke and my ankle swell,
it may get better, but I won't get well.
King Buzzard – calling out another lie –
tricked me from the keeping ground,
made me taste salt water so I knew I'd die.
But still waters still there,
when I saw I was lost, I knew I was found.

Oh yes, we've walked troubled waters:
Brer Man fiddled to the distant sound
of the ancestors' muffled drum,
and you paid – close attention.
You heard their constant and whispered voices
through the hammer of the work song,
and the field holler's call.
The cry of the mockingbird
is the wordless groan of a stolen people,
who grieve through the sorrow songs
to moan
the provocation of the blues.
We are the children of disappointment.

Yes, our foot bone broke and our ankle swell,
we may get better, but will we ever get well?
When there's so many rivers we've crossed
which clockwise do we turn to retrace the sun?

You tracked your namesake down those southern roads
that enjoined no hiding place –
and it was tough.
You heard through the buoyancy of his high laughter
the protective voice of the high priest
or the timbre of a monk, intoning with grace
the sacred chants of value
hidden in the hearts of a people.

Yes, our foot bones broke and our ankles swell,
if we sing ourselves better, then we may get well.
Of our long line of prophet priests and priestly kings
who nursed the fires of ancestral spirits and taught us
to be good and conscious
that the soul of the race is made manifest
in the sounds we make and leave in our wake –
you teach us to 'hear the fierceness of their truth'
for the subtle architecture of our being is drawn
from parent to child in living communion;
from ancestors to heirs in constant conversation.

As we are climbing Jacob's ladder
with the burning fires of Joe Hill's commitment,
all yesterday's sermons become tomorrow's freedom songs:
You may bury me in the east
or you may bury me in the west
or you may help me
                    steal out of town.

This has been no festival, let's state the theme:
at this junction we stay loose when time is tight –
between the diminuendo of our justice
and the crescendo of our righteousness
we have improvised
a blues bridge for freedom.

So, the circle stays unbroken.
You have shouted out the rhythms of the beat
and taught the dance that marked it once for all
in the shuffled footfall of our swollen feet,
on the off beat may we answer to the call,

dear teacher, you have passed us your sword and shield
here at this riverside:
oh, our foot bones may break and our ankles may swell,
yet we sang ourselves better, watch we'll dance ourselves
    well.

                              UC Riverside, 22 May 2004.

27. Centenary Memory Beads for Mr Bunche: A Necklace of Words

(7 August 1904–9 December 1971)

For Mr Ralph Johnson Bunche, on the centenary of his birth –
What can be the generation of memory?
The stories are so many and so few,

From Pacific halls west to Atlantic plazas,
if we encircle the globe
what story beads can we tell?

What does it take to recollect a legacy so large,
to honour and to keep in mind
decades of public labour so invisible and private?

Let's tell the first bead for the ancestors:

Offspring of the free of spirit
whether slaves or freemen, maids or schoolmasters
his was an American life –

His inheritance a fierce love
that nurtured dignity and taught
the pride of doing all things well

And left as sweet and lasting legacy
a simple admonition
never to abandon faith, hope, and dreams.

Let's tell the second bead for the orphaned boy:

Who dreamed he'd walk the mountains
and claimed the whole broad world
his schoolroom;

For the twice valedictory dutiful son, who learned well
the lessons of his worth
that no barred swimming pools and closed Honour clubs

And segregated dining cars
could dishonour.
What rites of memory can we perform?

Let's tell the third bead for the scholar athlete:

Who loved hoops and laughter
and stowed away on ships,
who laid carpets, shelled peas,

And learned to sing the toreador's song
as well as the cabin boy's call.
Who upheld his life-long the dignity of labour,

And early claimed an Olympian call
of overarching sympathy
that like love creates new worlds from old.

So let's tell the fourth bead for the visionary:

Who first in so many things,
through silent protests and quiet pickets
and early direct action

Trekked across this land
and voyaged around the world
for all our civil rights and freedoms.

From DC to London, from Togo to Cape Town,
from Nairobi to Palestine, and back again,
what moments are there, for us to recall?

We'll tell the fifth bead for the scholar:

Who took a world-view on race,
and laid bare the foundations of this American dilemma
that ruled the nation and controlled the world.

What mementoes can be garnered
by those who never know him.
What rite of memory can be performed?

When memories begin to fade or falter coast to coast –
from towering building to sculpture park,
What is it they aim to recall?

Let's tell the sixth bead for the visionary diplomat:

Who helped transform the league of nations
into a more lasting union
when the world had had enough of war,

Who believed like the prophet we could indeed
beat swords into plough shares
and spears into pruning hooks.

What rite of memory can we implore
for a lifetime ensuring
we should study war no more?

So let's tell the seventh bead for the international servant:

Strong in spirit and bold of mind
whose métier was words
forged in chambers, bedrooms, and conference halls

To wake the nations,
some to rise and claim their seats
and some to lay their armour down.

What rites of memory can recall
the faithful Trustee whose negotiations were directed
towards mutual respect amongst peoples?

So tell the stories of the eighth bead of sacrifice:

For the man who knew both early and grown
too many losses,
of sudden deaths too young;

Who mourned mentors, colleagues, children, friends,
In the exacting toll of service
and never told the price he paid

For other people's treaties –
Who wrestled a truce with words – a new colossus
bestriding ancient gulfs.

So let's prize the ninth bead of the man of peace:

And the nobility of his prayer –
that there may be freedom and equality and independence won
for the brotherhood of nations;

That coming generations
may find the path to the simple hope
of a good life for all peoples,

And the right to walk with dignity
on all the world's great boulevards
'to make full use of the greater good that is in us'.

So we can call the last bead in simple dedication:
For Mr Ralph Johnson Bunche on the centenary of his birth –

UCLA 3 June, 2004.

28. Random Reminders of Sudden Mortality

(For Ariana Worthington Clarke Windle,
2 October 1951–20 August 2004)

Wednesday, 1 September, Murray Hall, Rutgers University,
College Avenue Campus
The new message on my machine
is a surprise
and so too Christina, the messenger, with her simple request
to call back

and so too her unencompassable message.

Wednesday, 8 September, George and Somerset Streets, New
Brunswick NJ
Like our conversations, my mind turns in sudden ways:
        we meet to take down certain curtains in my empty
        house
        in an English country village,
And taking tea on the bare floor traverse the world
        made by immigrants and Jews
        in turn-of-century Brooklyn.

The waters of the Gulf of Guinea and Chesapeake Bay
        entwined for a time through our shared lives
        on the banks of a Windrush village.
And now in this New Jersey valley, which through your sister
        We also share, but were never together.
        Except in my thoughts –

Here on this Wednesday morning
        in the midst of a rainstorm and the chaos
        of another funeral for the sudden dead,
My thoughts turn to you and yours.

*Wednesday 8 September, Hamilton St. and College Avenue, New
Brunswick NJ*
The Parish Church of St Giles, Patron Saint of strangers, will
be packed tomorrow,
      And I will not be there.
      For I am here
      on these New Brunswick streets,
      circumventing the traffic jam
Of state officials and fire chiefs parading to honour their
fallen brother.

The Church of St Giles, Patron Saint of Strangers, will be
packed tomorrow,
      And I think only as I navigate these streets
      seeking parking on a day of threatening storm,
      of the disruptions of the elements,
      and random mortality
And the bravery of your suddenly orphaned children.

'Her children are the same age as mine,' my sister-in-law's
lament
      hovered over our plans to mourn you.
      She tomorrow in the English Cotswolds,
      me next month in the patrician Howard County;
      Hours later the tears in her voice slide down my face
as I slip into the only vacant parking space on these
disturbed streets.
Recalling we never, in the end, decided about the flowers.

*Wednesday, 8 September, Murray Hall, Rutgers University,
College Avenue Campus*
Back once more in this office, a vortex of silence like white noise
      Engulfs the memory of suffocation
      And imploding walls and severed phone calls
And the forceful denials that sent me hurtling through these
corridors.

As if the fury of a choking grief could unsay words, could recall time.

>Loss collapses in on us in silly details
>*like the last email I never answered, and the call I didn't make*
And how did your children find my office number?

Is the wrought iron gate you rescued from my now sold home
>still in your back field? *And how your steel blue eyes were*
>*so watchful*
>And was the death certificate issued in time
for a funeral tomorrow? And which train will Monica catch?

'The saintly Monica' as you once called her, introduced us
>in a simple act of kindness as she knew we'd be friends
>*and how your watchful eyes were tender*
And how surprisingly soft your well-cut and your still unruly hair
was.

As I allow Christina's voice to be erased from my answering machine,
>I see still posted on the Oxford Arts and Culture
>websites
>The advertisements for the workshops you were to do
>this month.
Yet your grip was firm and the set of your smiling mouth was
strong.

I remember the moment I noticed the strength of your muscled painter's fingers.
>You were drawing my portrait in pastels
>and I thought how their tight look belied
the softness of your touch in every gesture of comfort or gentle reassurance.

Saturday, 2 October, on an Amtrak train north from Metropark NJ.
Today would have been, is, will always be, your birthday.
>And I travel in this limbo zone from one state to another
>to celebrate the birthdays of other friends;
>one, eight years younger than you,
>the other seven years older
who are both alive to greet this weekend.

One week today, I will be on these same tracks riding in the
opposite direction
>with other friends to mourn you,
>who are at home in so many places.
>We will all pass away, Ariana,
>but why our friend, this sudden parting, this soon?
As we prepare another form of celebration, accept this our
last gift,

Though no wreath of words can portrait as generous
>as the gifts you left for us in ink, and paint, and
>pastels. Once
>tributes to the interiors and landscapes you grew to
>love. Now
Mementos for those of us you touched in your sharing of all
that beauty.

Mourning is unendurable, and can only be survived through
routine acts of dedication,
>so the mosaic triptych you designed of salvaged tiles
>is completed and installed on our riverbank: *In
>memoriam
Eternal. Your last still life.

Clarkesville VA, 9 October 2004.

29. Titles for Wesley Brown: Take Two

(For Wesley, to Acknowledge, Reluctantly, His Retirement)

Be assured, we *will* talk about you when you're gone,
about how your mojo was your say so
and what you said , and how you said it.

Talking like you got books in your jaws,
you followed your own law –
'don't just sit here, create!'

And you gave us plays – and disquisitions
in all your many voices.
You listened in our cities of noise

To bring us stories of our promised lands;
Where push always came to shove
in the places of our visions and imaginings;

Where darktown strutters shed minstrel masks,
and murderesses loved, and claimed life during wartime:
   boogie woogie, boogie woogie woogie

Through your life, in your life
what is tragic turns to magic
for you teach, because you learned

That the important part of life
is the jam session of the middle distance –
if we stay loose when time is tight.

Note: 'mojo' is a slang word for magic (often black magic) "your mojo was
your say so" is, like everyline in the poem, a reference to a title of one of
Wesley's essays. In US slang to say something is someone's "say so" is to
emphasise that that is their way, and their last word.

So in the land of *oh-bla-dee* the bands play on,
blowing our song – we had a prophet among,
and he left us, laughing 'I was here, but I disappeared.'

Rutgers, 30 March 2005.

30. Ancestral Milk

(For Miriam Nkiado Traditional Priestess, Salaga, Ghana)

i. White Calico
Beyond the market
on the outskirts of Salaga,
in what used to be wilderness,
you will find a solitary baobab tree,
wrapped in white calico
in a vegetable garden planted with corn.

Baobab trees are sacred;
they grow large, live long
and are strong,
strong enough to contain the spirits of ancestors
and the unquiet dead.
White calico rings this ancient tree of accidental sanctity
where the dead en route were dumped.
Not buried, but deposited as refuse
beside the still living abandoned dying,
chained by the neck to the trunk.
Through the centuries, bark has encrusted the iron staples
like scabs over sores,
obscuring the cause of the infection with a scaly patina
gnarled by time and circumstance and silent sorrow.

ii. White Beads
A priestess, the white beads of office on her neck and wrists,
tends to the crop to keep the garden tidy.
Interrupted, she pauses to explain
the functions of her office:
Every Friday and every Monday, year after year
she nourishes spirits with milk,
to keep them safe
under this tree,

performing her lonely office
of tending the unmarked graves
of the abandoned dead of unknown family,
feeding fresh milk to the spirits of captives
who died walking to or marching from
this market of slaves.
Every Friday and every Monday

Through the centuries,
while Muslims raided the peoples to the north
and sold them to the Christians in the south
her family of traditional priests have fed the spirits of the
    dead.
And continue to do so long after the trade in flesh has stopped
and Muslims and Christians trade peacefully
in whatever new commodity needs exchanging in their age –
gold, gunpowder, kola nuts,
leather goods, fabrics, second-hand car parts.

What is the depth of anguish, and what the faith
that commits mother, sister, daughter, niece
week in week out, through the centuries,
to perform this lonely office
unwitnessed, unsupported, unacknowledged.

iii. White Milk
Once this was wilderness, and foreboding forest,
where vultures preyed on the bones of those
who would not be missed, or could never be found.
But these women found you, and knew someone would miss
    you.

Too late to tend to your bodies,
year after year they nourish your spirits with milk,
to keep you safe under this tree.
For fed spirits can be satiated and made happy;
can be made to dance under the protection of these branches.

So here, in a place where named ancestors
drink greedily, the clear spirits poured
by those of their own blood,
you unnamed lost spirits
crave cow's milk for food
in your limbo of time.

So come, eat, you who marched the trail of tears and died here;
you the rebellious and you the weak,
come, eat, you whose spirits were broken by the flesh
     markets and the forts;
you the heroic and you the conspirators,
come, eat you who tried to just make a way to live, and faltered.

You of unnameable ancestors, and unknown descendants,
     come
Here, after all, you are safe.
Here every Friday and every Monday
one woman at a time, through the centuries, has prayed for
     you,
has fed you milk under a baobab tree scarred by your iron
and swathed in calico to greet you through the centuries
unwitnessed, unacknowledged, unmemorialised.

Salaga, Ghana, 9 July 2005.
Bellagio, Italy, 1 September 2005.

68

31. Pieta

(Toby Lund Schroeder, 7 March 2001–3 December 2005:
In Cherished Memory,)
(For Do and Rick and Luke)

Words Fail.
Those of us who love you agonize in advance
Over the inadequate language of sorrow.

We wrestle for courage to meet you and say, what, exactly?
That we are sorry for the loss
Of your bright, bright child of joyous earnestness,

last seen, by me, on a sofa, steadying a too large book
grasped precariously on his little lap, exposing
naked knees and knuckles beneath the hard open covers;

That we share the trauma of this, your darkest hour
When in truth, the terror of his loss
Is unimaginable.

In struggling moments of prayer
We defray facing your grief
By resisting comprehension.

Wordless we take solace in simple gestures
Of everyday ritual, and those images of you
We must confront and name:

Richard, whose very name means brave,
Finding the power to hold in immediate, in intense, anguish
The now dying, now dead, body of your last born, and
                                        Lay his body down.
Dorothy, the gift of God to him,
Who cradled your man-child to your breast,
To exchange too soon his baby blanket for a winding sheet.

You two it is who named him –
Toby, Tobias, To'bi'Jah,
God is Good.

As we all believed it then,
May we believe it now.
This is our prayer.

We labour in trust to birth our resolutions, and
Luke, bringer of sacramental light
Is the great physician of healing –

In struggle, you release who you were, and craft a new
    becoming,
And hold him dear as he holds treasure,
the playful brother of his eternal heart.

One word yet:
Next time I take my leave of a child
Whose very life I cherish,

I won't just wave at his swiftly departing back,
I'll take the time to touch him, as I

                                            Say Goodbye.

Rutgers, New Brunswick NJ, 14 December 2005.

32. Tectonics

(For Alero Olympio, 31 May 1959–23 August 2005)

After all, space
Is what you loved best.
And so, to make it dance in time with light,
You built your homes
To set space free.

Child of earth and air,
You made your walls slip
Out of sight
To rest with rocks.

And sound the sands you shaped,
Or soar to speak with sage old trees
Through that flash of love
That turns insight
To sight and touch.

Creation is a gift of time, however short;
So your tensile spirit lives
In your loving care for details.
The design of a corner, a kiss;
Arches framed through a window, a smile;
And a splash of unexpected colour,
A burst of primary laughter through silent, searing pain.

You knew proportion, a living skill,
And balance an act of claiming life:
Caught in camera flash and memory,
The art of ethical habitation your legacy
Of the way you walked this earth and stood your ground,
Firm, and gentle, and upright.

Kokrobitey, Ghana, 1 January 2006.

33. To the RoadMaker:
Fragments of a Meditation

(For Efua Theodora Sutherland on the Tenth Anniversary
of her passing)

January 21 2006, Accra, Ghana.

In this "over programmed" (how useful that word of yours is!) week of things to do, that has taken me from the inauguration of Ellen Johnson Sirleaf as President in Monrovia, to lectures to students from Rome in Kokrobitey, to lunches with students and friends from New Jersey it comes as a shock that ten years have gone by, already.

April 28 2006, New Brunswick NJ.

Today is my birthday, and in the midst of the celebrations for another poet, colleague Alicia Ostriker, I am holding my breath to tell my in-coming sister of the sudden death of Joe Ampah in Ghana yesterday. Some deaths come sudden, some like yours, come slow. Ten years ago I was with your Sisters Vivian Windley and Maya Angelou, doing our best to celebrate *you* at the tribute at the Schomburg. I performed the ending of Foriwa I had arranged for solo voice and drummer. Of all your works that is the one I love, whether as a story or as a play, the faith in 'New Life' that is based on seeing again, seeing differently what we do, what women do and have the courage to take on. Transformations, that is what you understood: 'Anansesem' into 'Anansegoro'; *Playtime in Africa* into the Mmofra Foundation; the inspiration of FESTAC into the establishment of PANAFEST; like your own Queenmother you built on old familiar rituals to make everything new again.

May 18 2006, Accra, Ghana.

Watching this production of *The Marriage of Anansewaa* during the return of the African Literature Association Conference to Accra, I can't help but remember that twelve years ago you were here with us. Thanks to your daughters, the production is another wonderful witness to your work. They have organised a glorious anniversary of productions of your plays. This time we also honoured your memory as we launched volume two of *Women Writing Africa*, at the Du Bois Centre. How very appropriate a confluence for the many reaches of your work. You supported the creation of that memorial space to that great Pan Africanist and helped bring it into being, and let me here put on record: you were the first of our literary foremothers to lend your name to our efforts to create our own monumental work to ourselves. Twelve years after you spoke in Accra then came to Rutgers to speak publicly about why that project which we were just undertaking, was important, the second volume on "West Africa and Sahel" is out, co-edited by your first-born Esi no less, isn't that great! We should have dedicated that volume to you. We have two volumes left to go, and it has been hard; your active encouragement was such an impetus to us at the start. You knew road-making is both exciting, and arduous- by the time it is done it will have taken nearly twenty years of my working life.

May 27 2006, Accra, Ghana.

I had drinks with Esi and Amowi, last night, enjoying music in the "African Village" Restaurant at La Palm in Accra. Like your children, of the body, of the stage, and of the story, who worked with and remember you, I too have much to thank you for. I can give so little back; the voice on the record of *Voice in the Forest* is mine, as is the music of the band we were listening to. It was such a joy to work with Esi and Amowi on that recording. Like us for our father, your children are working hard to give a firm foundation to your legacy. Your daughters are my friends now, though I knew you before I knew them, though they are my age. And strangely enough, I felt I knew you long before I ever met you, just because I loved your work. But it isn't ever that simple; you were not real, or, only as real as any writer we admire through their work – the familiarity of their words gives the illusion of a personal intimacy that doesn't exist. Then, imagine my shock to learn that Ayi Kwei Armah's "Akosua Russell" was supposedly a satire of you! Him, I had met, you I had not. His words were angry, but he himself seems gentle. So did your gently inspiring words mask a ruthlessness as fierce as his portrait? All this gave a sense of discomfort and split affinities; if that were you, how could we possibly wish to like you? The truth is, most of the time you were becoming YOU, I was a child, and away. The glory days of your early work, when you planted the seeds of so much we reap today, I was not here; those were the years of our first exile. Still even as a child I discovered you because someone, I don't know who, sent us, in England, a copy of *The RoadMakers*. I should know who it was, for in those days few people sent us anything out of Ghana. It was a precious gift, treasured along with a copy of *Panoply of Ghana*, random issues of *Okyeame* and the original *Transition*, and other such tokens from people who thought we should have other news than that of imprisoned and dying friends from home.

June 27 2006, Accra, Ghana.

Then I met you and realised what the satire lacked was your ability to give comfort and spread genuine laughter. And I grew to love your children whose elegant and simply appropriate resting place for you I have just left behind to come and sit with my own mother, beside her hospital bed. I hold her hand as she sleeps, conscious of the fragility of our lives- she was born the same year as you, and tenuous as her laboured breathing seems on this particular day, she is still here with us. All this has made this writing hard; like so much of my work over the last ten years it has been started and stopped too many times. I promised it to Esi, and have not been able to finish it in time for her festschrift.

Coda

What is there to say? You have left large footprints and we are still trying to sort out where some of them might lead. Nana Ayebia Clarke my Publisher insisted that whatever I have drafted, I must hand over to her to put with the rest of my elegies and praise poems because you deserved no less!

I have tried to keep living, one breath at a time, one line at a time. These memories are not all what I wanted to say, nor these halting fragments how I wanted to say it. It is simply what is left of the tears I could not shed, the dance I could not come to dance, and the poem I could not write.

June 27 2008, New Brunswick, NJ.

34. Notes for a Composition for Peggy Friedman

(18 August 1949–8 February 2006)

Sunlight slices through half-open window blinds
pouring darkness and light on your partially stripped bed;
Packed boxes stand by the door at the ready;
You are moving home on the eve of your marriage.
The African violet on the sill seems conscious
of the slow accretion of signs of imminent change.

Myself a recent arrival, I am here, helping you pack.
You let me keep the solitary violet.

On that day of incomplete transitions, the half-tuned radio
transmits, now clear, now crackled, a set of competing
    signals;
Fundamentalist preachers sow words of potential discord
against the soothing background of harmonious hymns;
And on Pacifica radio, turbulent voices rise in conflict
as if drafting a search for inclusive solutions.

Folding sheets, your activism and my faith move together
enveloping each other in the contrariness of friendships, and
    life.

You taught on how to grapple with the complexity of
    questions
that light us through opaque Americas of dreams, and brutal
    realities:
If no words speak self-evident truths of religion, being, or
    class,
What then is the lesson of race at the end of history?
Who is the model minority in this republic of privilege?
How to create, and create again, a community?

This a composition assignment, however difficult,
First, please, define a thesis statement.

For you, each age brought its own new commitments,
And rough, life became a perpetual revision towards clarity.
From Cape Town to Baghdad or Cape May to Piscataway,
You chose your community and joined the call to account:
For one warmonger to trust peace, or one uncertain voter
to defy complacency, march, or take a stand.

To transform a nation, or one life, like parsing meaning,
takes care, and much wry commitment.

I once saw you in the doorway of your home, your body
     wracked with pain,
Smiling, as sunlight burst in on the rubber plant you once took
To tend for me while on leave. In two decades, I never took it
     back.
It thrived in that entrance, out-growing its pot, its corner, and
     each of us.
Living things struggle to survive, all eventually die.
What matters are the journeys that make dark places bright:

How you so loved this life lived in sunlight and shadow.
This, at last, is my thesis statement for you.

Accra – Ghana, 2 April 2006.

35. Seventeen Syllables
to Keep a Promise

(For Joseph Erskine Ampah: 24 February 1954–27 April 2006)

The clock stopped by three.
Comprehension shocked the dawn,
by this hour, you'd died.

Washington DC, 28 April 2006.

36. Between Faith and History

*(For President John Agyekum Kufuor at the Launch of Between
Faith and History: A Biography of J.A. Kufuor: first published by
Ayebia Clarke Publishing Limited, 2006)*

Faith has insights history cannot explain,
And we, mere mortals, strive to trace
The course of destiny
Backwards to its source
And craft explanations of endings
Only prophets – or mothers, can divine:
Sankofa.

This is the story of a tenacious man
In whom lineage bred a commitment to service,
And heritage became that fierce force of loyalty
That forges that enduring will to be.

To be, and be here now
Avuncular mentors taught passion, taught courage,
And much, much patience.
They held out hands to walk those same long roads uphill
That turned down and around again,
Through palaces and porters' lodges
Through prison cells to castles,
Where friend and foe alike
Have equal access to your days.

For between being and destiny
Lies only that will to be, and be free:
And history is a worthy path
We can only walk through faith.

La-Palm Royal Beach Hotel,
Accra, 10 January, 2007.

37. One Last Embrace
for Auntie Mercy

*(For Mercy Adebi Busia, Mother of Bra' Kwesi,
11 November 1919–31 May 2007)*

To show mercy we touch,
A head, a face, a hand;
In holding hands we claim each other;

This I learned as a little girl,
Grasping your skirt as we stood on trembling earth
As the flood waters rose.

Uncurling my tremulous clutch
You held my small hand, firmly, but gently, in yours
As we crossed the breached and broken wall,
In an intricate dance.

For you, once, dancing was the business of life.
Stormy life was joyous as your dance partner became your
    life partner.
Then you learned to hold each other and *pas de deux*
When the music stopped –

And through long dirge years of sudden separations
Of families fractured by jail, by exile,
And the shattering, searing pain of the passing of the
    firstborn
You exchanged your lilac gowns for indigo cloth.

Yet still, through all, to shepherd children; to Homes; to shelter,
Remained your special care.
Unheralded and obedient to your life in prayer
You trusted encounters with strangers and joined a
     movement -S.O.S-
To create a net to pull the children to shore,
As years ago you delivered me, home
to the arms of my waiting mother.

Ma, Auntie, Teacher Mercy,
The God who named you, has claimed you
To take you safely Home,
Like all those children who felt your touch
Like a firmly grasped hand through a storm.

Accra, 28 July 2007.

38. Still Morning Yet

(For Chinua Achebe on the Fiftieth Anniversary of Things Fall Apart)

He is well known throughout the seven continents
And even beyond.
His fame rests on solid personal achievements.
Fifty years ago he brought honour to his people
By conjouring up the man who could throw Amalinze the
    Cat.
This much we can say:

Through him we have learned
Balance is necessary, but difficult.
His progeny all of us,
No longer at ease in any dispensations
Old or new, for the arrows of old gods
Full of hope, still meet impediments;
Like a man of the people we must learn
What the trouble is with us.
And the lessons do not fail.

In the ageless cycle of the time of the anthills
He records new poems in an ancient language;
In the evening wisdom of encroaching Savannahs
He crafts new language for old stories;
As the moon encircles the changing earth
Our stories must map uncharted territories
And though some died in his shadow, many others thrived
Because he showed us a way:

Things are coming together
Our hero Okonkwo is fifty
And in the measure of creation day
And the time of the classics
It is still yet morning.

Accra, Ghana, July 2008.

39. Postlude: What is Africa to Me?
Knowledge Possession, Knowledge Production, and the Health of Our Bodies

At home Death claims
Two streams from women's eyes
And many day-long dirges;
Gnashes, red eyes and sighs from men,
The wailing of drums and muskets
And a procession of the townsfolk
Impeded
Only if the coffin decides
To take one last look at the home.

But here I see
Three cars in procession.
The first holds three –
A driver chatting gaily with a mate,
And behind them, flowers on a bier.
The second holds five, and the third too.
A procession
Efficiently arranged by the undertaker,
From the brass fittings on the bier
To the looks of sorrow on the mourners' faces.
And Death is escorted
Tearlessly but efficiently
By
Three cars in procession.

Jawa Apronti, "Funeral"

Funerals are important,
away from home we cannot lay
our dead to rest,
for we alone have given them
no fitting burial.

Self conscious of our absence,
brooding over distances in Western lands
we must rehearse,
the planned performance of our rites
till we return.

And meanwhile through the years,
our unburied dead eat with us,
follow behind through bedroom doors
                            Abena P. A. Busia, "Exiles".

In 1976, in the middle of what was for us a second exile, my
father's younger brother died. This death was shortly followed
by the news of the death of his 112-year-old aunt, the only
grandmother we had ever known. In accordance with custom
and tradition, a few weeks later, and against the odds, the
family in Wenchi, a town in the Brong-Ahafo region in the
middle of Ghana, managed to send to Papa in Standlake, a
small village in the countryside west of Oxford, the fragment of
the burial cloth that was his aunt's and which he would have
received on the day of the burial, had he been there. My father
had by then lost his sight, but the strip of cloth was put in his
hand, and he kept it in his bedside drawer until the day he too
went home to his village. When it was given to him, I watched
him fingering it over and over and over again, in complete
silence. I left him sitting on his bed, fingering that strip in a
lonely pensiveness, and was moved to write my poem "Exiles."
Funerals *are* important, and that was the moment I learnt just
how important they were. That poem became the first of my
poems I ever read to my father (though there had been many

others written earlier). It thus also became the poem which made my father aware that, and express his consciousness of the fact that, his political decisions had affected us, his children, so very personally, in ways he had never realised or antici- pated. That is the private face of death from the perspective of exile, and is only one of the generative threads or colours with which these meditations begin. There are many threads running through these remarks I share with you this evening – the question of rituals of mourning is one, the meaning of those practices for those of Diasporas old and new is another.

That as communities of learning we are now strategically aware of the need for African studies to be at the centre of Diaspora studies and for Disapora studies to be integral to African studies is absolutely critical. But these days, we are increasingly aware of multiple Diaspora, including what some people in short-hand call old Disapora and new Disapora. The old Diaspora centred on the forced migrations of the transat- lantic slave trade and the new worlds it created, and the new Diaspora on much more recent immigrants, those post–World War II migrants who represent the continuing power differen- tial between "the West and the Rest of Us," in a long continuum of human exchange; we are the flotsam and jetsam of other traumatic moments: same story, different century.

The extent to which it is the same story I can perhaps bring out most clearly by asking you to imagine Ganvie, one of the villages built on water which, as the work of scholars such as Eliseé Soummoni has shown us, formed part of the intricate network of defence devised in resistance to the trade. If we wish to have a discussion about how groups respond to centuries of sustained terror, a trip I took last summer was a salutary reminder of a wealth of those strategies, from the walled cities of Gwellu, to the architecture of the Paga Piiu's palace, to these villages in the network of lagoons in the Bight of Benin. Imagine on those waters not only the fishermen touted to us as picturesque in poverty by a rapacious tourist industry, but also traffic of long motorised barges loaded with empty black oil drums, piled high on top of one another headed for Lagos to collect contraband oil. And it hit me, for the first time, that slavery was a *trade*. That is to say, as someone in the humanities, I had always looked at the slave trade from the point of view of the moral issue of slavery. That single vision of the oil from Lagos being smuggled through that same ancient network of lagoons that a little over a century ago facilitated the illegal trade in human traffic impressed upon me more fully than any other words or images that slavery truly was a trade, a trade which, given the organisation of the economies of the day, was as life sustaining for the participant communities as illegal oil is today. For the flesh that is black ivory substitute the liquid that is black gold: same story, different century; same business, different product.

I'm concerned also, as are all of us in this room, with the larger context in which we recognise that very often African knowledge is surreptitious knowledge as far as the Western world is concerned. The history of power and imperialism and colonialism has given rise to a world in which it is not possible to be in African and Diaspora studies and be unaware of the questions and problems posed by the seeming contradictions between Western cultural and economic imperialism and black / African cultural identities, but the reverse is not true. We have not reversed the power differentials between the "West and the Rest of Us," and in the immediate centuries that shape the lives we live today, that struggle for power has been an unequal one at every level.

It would he satisfying if at this juncture I could follow these opening comments by offering a grand narrative of postcolonial discourse which would place us firmly in a coherent universe of explanations. It would be comforting to have a vision of Africa to go "back" to, to explain our new world agonies in terms of old world certainties. But if those worlds ever existed, they certainly are not there now. I offer, therefore, no grand narratives, only the exemplary moments of poetry. I am, if you like, a poet of the freeze frame, in close up. I offer a handful of memories, frozen in poetic time for contemplation, to see if we can understand them for the complexity of what they represent, in miniature.

I opened this talk with two poems. And the parallel between the situations of their opening lines was not accidental. Jawa Appronti's poem is a poem spoken by a person clearly in exile; entitled "Funeral," it begins with the words. "At *home* death." My poem, entitled "Exile" begins with the words "*funerals* are important." In Apronti's poem the speaker is not actually in the process of mourning; what the poem does is point out a context, which is so evident to a Ghanaian, concerning modes of mourning and the rituals associated with it. He articulates those "absences in distant lands" to which I refer. What I am conscious of is not even simply the existence of different kinds of funerals so much as the absence of the expression of a particular kind of public solidarity in, and expression of, grief. That expression represented by the townsfolk of Apronti's poem: we are removed from all of it. That is the thing that struck me about the question of rituals of mourning and therefore the impact of grief when you are in exile. Both poems interrogate the meaning of life, and thus the meaning of death – and in their very existence, the purpose of poetry. Poetry and ritual, in this case the poetry of mourning and the rituals associated with it, do bear witness, but what kind of witness is it that they bear?

My father, the Ghanaian sociologist K. A. Busia, opened his book *The Challenge of Africa* (1962), one of his two books on Africa in search of democracy, with an extended discussion of "culture," beginning with a discussion of funeral practices because his research had shown him that "the study of rituals and beliefs connected with the dead became rewarding as a means of understanding their concepts of life and their interpretation of the universe around them."

There is, everywhere, the heavy accent on family – the blood relatives, the group of kinsfolk held together by a common origin and a common obligation to its members, to those who are living and those who are dead. For the family is conceived as consisting of a large number of people, many of whom are dead, a few of whom are living, and countless numbers of whom are yet to be born.... Belief in the continuity of the family lies at the basis of obligation, of law and custom, of behaviour. It guides and regulates individual conduct. The ancestors continue as members of the group. They watch over it. [However], the death of a member is the concern not only of the king-group but of the whole village or [tribal] community. Normal activities are suspended; everyone joins in the mourning; in the wailing and drumming and dancing. The cost to the community in time and economic production may be heavy, but the community's values are not measured thus.

These values are expressed within the ceremonies, as an integral part of the rituals and the dirges. Death is a part of the cycle of creation, yet it is painful because it is separation, particularly to those closest to the deceased. This pain is thus both expressed and exorcised through the performance of the elaborate rituals of each part of the three- or four-part funeral rituals. We know the deceased must "go home" to join the ancestors to continue to watch over us, but it is hard to see them go. We are enjoined not to wail, but the wailing is an integral part of the ceremonies. These observations have most meaning in the context in which they are offered, in a vital recognition of different rituals of mourning. Both the physical and the metaphysical worlds are thrown into disarray when death occurs.

The poignancy of the sight of Father at his most alone, stroking his aunt's burial cloth, comes from a recognition that for him, his exile meant the absence of the performance of ritual, an absence of ritual which, for him, was a total disruption of what Carolyn Forché calls his "moral universe" (2000: 45), in which ritual observation was a part of the moral framework of ontological order. Those rituals anchor the sense of identity and human community (he was the first-born son of the only sister, and considered the head of the family); his world had been rendered askew, and he could not play his part in setting it aright. In the end, Father never returned to do that. He died in exile, in August of 1978, and was given, under difficult circumstances, a state funeral in October 1978, forty days after his passing. His family, having waited through the years for him to return for the final funeral rites, held joint ceremonies for him, his aunt, and his younger brother the following spring. This is the context in which Apronti's poem must be heard. Apronti's poem, written and read in circumstances in which the meanings of funerals are so different, attempts to anchor a sense of the politics of cultural difference for survivors and other displaced, exiled peoples. My sense of the word *exile* is of course, by virtue of biography, political exile. However, I wish to stress that I would like to embrace all forms of involuntary displacement, whether for reasons of politics and war, or for those equally forceful, equally involuntary, but less readily demonstrable reasons – economic and social. And propitiation must be made to set all worlds aright.

That propitiation goes beyond the personal. On my trip last summer, one of the most significant stops on the route was Salaga, the site of the ancient market. In that place we met a woman, whose story is self-explanatory:

Ancestral Milk

i. White Calico
Beyond the market
on the outskirts of Salaga,
in what used to be wilderness,
you will find a solitary baobab tree,
wrapped in white calico

in a vegetable garden planted with corn.
Baobab trees are sacred
they grow large, live long
and are strong
strong enough to contain the spirits of ancestors
and the unquiet dead.
White calico rings this ancient tree of accidental sanctity
where the dead en route were dumped.
Not buried, but deposited as refuse
beside the still living abandoned dying,
chained by the neck to the trunk.
Through the centuries bark has encrusted the iron staples
like scabs over sores
obscuring the cause of the infection with a scaley patina
gnarled by time and circumstance and silent sorrow.

ii. White Beads
A priestess, the white beads of office on her neck and wrists
tends to the crop to keep the garden tidy.
Interrupted, she pauses to explain
the functions of her office:
Every Friday and Every Monday, year after year
she nourishes spirits with milk,
to keep them safe
under this tree,
performing her lonely office
of tending the unmarked graves
of the abandoned dead of unknown family
feeding fresh milk to the spirits of captives
who died walking to or marching from
this market of slaves.
Every Friday and every Monday
Through the centuries,
while Muslims raided the peoples to the north
and sold them to the Christians in the south
her family of traditional priests have fed the spirits of the dead.

And continue to do so long after the trade in flesh has
stopped
and Muslims and Christians trade peacefully
in whatever new commodity needs exchanging in their age-
gold, gunpowder, kola nuts,
leather goods, fabrics, second hand car parts.

What is the depth of anguish, and what the faith
that commits mother, sister, daughter niece
week in week out, through the centuries,
to perform this lonely office
unwitnessed, unsupported, unacknowledged.

iii. White Milk
Once this was wilderness, and foreboding forest
where vultures preyed on the bones of those
who would not be missed, or could never be found.
But these women found you, and knew someone would miss
    you.

Too late to tend to your bodies,
year after year they nourish your spirits with milk,
to keep you safe under this tree.
For fed spirits can be satiated and made happy,
can be made to dance under the protection of these branches.

So here, in a place where named ancestors
drink greedily the clear spirits poured
by those of their own blood,
you unnamed lost spirits
crave cow's milk for food
in your limbo of time.

So come, eat, you who marched the trail of tears and died here;
you the rebellious and you the weak,
come, eat, you whose spirits were broken by the flesh
    markets and the forts;
you the heroic and you the conspirators,
come, eat you who tried to just make a way to live, and
    faltered.

You of unnameable ancestors, and unknown descendants,
    come
Here, after all, you are safe.
Here every Friday and every Monday
one woman at a time, through the centuries, has prayed for
    you
has fed you milk under a baobab tree scarred by your iron
and swathed in calico to greet you through the centuries
unwitnessed, unacknowledged, unmemorialized.

                    Salaga, July and September 1, 2005.

In all the disruptions of history, there are multiple groups of people left trying to restore a sense of order, those for whom here and there, then and now, are not so easily divided. What persists is the need to bear witness.

In her introduction to *Against Forgetting: Twentieth-Century Poetry of Witness* (2000), Carolyn Forché says of the poets in her anthology that they are those for whom:

> the social had been irrevocably invaded by the political in ways that were sanctioned neither by law nor by the fictions of the social contract,… those for whom the normative promises of the nation-state have failed. They have not been afforded the legal or physical protections that the modern state is supposed to lend its citizens. Nor have they been able to enjoy the solidarity that the concept of the nation is supposed to provide.

She is speaking, in this case, of those who had suffered internal displacements and the brutalities of the state – often including imprisonment, torture, and death – enacted against its own citizens who did not manage to get away. Yet that statement can also be said to be true of those of us who did manage to make it out, and who never suffered such brutalities; those who nonetheless remain migrants of tragedy rather than (necessarily) migrants of adversity.

Forché goes on to point out that:

> Poetry of witness presents the reader with an interesting interpretive problem. We are accustomed to rather easy categories: we distinguish between "personal" and "political" poems – the former calling to mind lyrics of love and emotional loss, the latter indicating a public partisanship that is considered divisive, even when necessary. The distinction between the personal and the political gives the political realm too much and too little scope; at the same time, it renders the personal too important and not important enough. If we give up the dimension of the personal, we risk relinquishing one of the most powerful sites of resistance. The celebration of the personal, however, can indicate a myopia, an inability to see how larger structures of the economy and the state circumscribe, if not determine, the fragile realm of individuality.

She therefore proposes a third term that can, as she puts it, "describe the space between the state and the supposedly safe havens of the personal". She calls this space the "social", for "the social is a place of resistance and struggle, where books are published, poems read, and protest disseminated. It is the sphere in which claims against the political order are made in the name of justice."

The poems I offer are precisely those that have arisen out of those junctures, moments in which poetry offers itself up, in the name of justice, to grapple with a disordered world in the context of saving rituals. But first, another anecdote.

A few years ago I was invited to the Rochester Institute of Technology to conduct a faculty development workshop. So whilst there, I took the opportunity of visiting the Eastman Kodak Museum. I was fortunate that it was the year of the centenary of the Brownie, and amongst the many events celebrating that little camera, which was the first camera of almost everyone I know, was a glorious exhibit of every Brownie ever made, displayed in chronological order. We could all mark our age group by the camera we first knew. What was very striking was that if you looked at only the first and the last in the series, the two cameras had nothing in common. Yet when they were seen on display, with the dozens of intervening cameras also displayed, it was clear that the differences between each that had led to such a large change overall were only small and incremental, at times barely perceptible, and the links between the cameras at their different stages were irrefutable.

It might be fruitful to think of that vexed word *tradition* in the same manner. With each manifestation of a "traditional" ceremony, what is produced is its own variant, dependent on its own time, space, and ritual acts and immediate needs. Nothing remains static; the way we mourn and perform our rituals for the dead in New Jersey is not the way we do it in Wenchi. This is the health of ritual. However, in form and performance, rituals still carry the echo of that remembered form which each performance both recalls and gives life to. So instead of sitting in open spaces outside the family home, we hire church halls and do the things that need to be done, improvising from necessity to create something new that we dress in the language of tradition, sometimes amazing and bemusing our neighbours because of the sudden influx of people and colour, all the public ceremony and noise that

Ghanaian funerals generate, which seem incomprehensible unless you understand the culture of mourning. The danger is the extent to which we are all capable of amnesia, forgetting the cameras in between.

As Isidore Okpewho (1979, 1990, 1992) and others have pointed out, much of African oral performance poetry occupies this space of the social, sometimes as resistance, and sometimes as celebration. This is particularly true of dirges and lamentations. In many African societies – and I speak here particularly of Akan society – death, which signifies a transition from this world into that of the ancestors, is a time of collective mourning and celebration. Whole communities mourn because death curtails people's contributions to individual and community lives. However, the belief that existence continues in the spiritual world of the ancestors, from where the spirits can and do commune with the living, enables communities to celebrate death. In funeral and burial ceremonies, meant to usher the deceased into their next abode, much of the expression of grief is channelled through the aesthetically controlled mode of songs, chants, and recitatives, performed at different and sometimes dramatic points of the ceremony, such as the moment the wake begins. Ceremonies also play an important role of historical record-keeping, since they function as texts that place the dead person's life in social and historical perspective. In what follows, the need is to remember that sameness in difference, that shift with every repetition that makes each individualised act sacred in itself, yet comprehensible in a larger context.

Ghanaian funeral rituals include, particularly for public occasions, many kinds of eulogising acts, and here I need to speak of one of the first of them as a force that inspired me to write one of my poems into that space of the social where poems are produced for performance. We have become accustomed to the convention that obituaries are what we read in the newspapers and include in the burial service: a brief encapsulation of the major events of the deceased's life by which we should remember the person. But this is not the actual meaning of the word. The word simply means a report of a death, and Ghanaian funeral announcements are just that, but in an elaborate and stylised way.

Our obituary notices are large public announcements, notices on A3 paper, in a recognisable format. At the very top will be the leading members of the deceased person's lineage on both sides of the family, and the announcement that such and such personages, of such and such a family, regret to announce the calling home of their beloved such and such. And it will be followed by a photograph, the name and the dates of the deceased, the dates of the wake ceremonies, the burial, funeral, and memorial services, and then a list of the other members of the lineages (aunts and uncles, brothers and sisters, children and in-laws, grandchildren, nephews and nieces) and the chief mourners – such people as are significant to the life and ceremonies though they may not necessarily be blood relations. These obituaries are just that, announcements of a death which then become not a recital of the achievements of the life (that is done at another place and time), but rather an archaeology of family and community, locating the deceased person in his or her distinct lineages and communal associations.

Now one of the things that impelled me to write the poem "And What Remains" for the funeral of General A. A. Afrifa was a sharp moment of poignancy and pathos on reading his particular funeral announcement in January 2002. General Afrifa, best known for being one of the people who spearheaded the coup against Nkrumah (thus making it possible for us to return home after our first exile), had later become chairman of the three-man Presidential Commission before the selection of Edward Akufo-Addo as civilian president of the Second Republic, of which my father was the prime minister. After the coup which overthrew the Second Republic (and sent us into our second exile), Afrifa was one of the principal agitators for the return of the Third Republic. He never lived to see it, for he was one of the people rounded up in the so-called Glorious Revolution of Jerry Rawlings (in his first dispensation, as head of state, as Flight Lieutenant Rawlings) in June 1979, and along with six other officers – two others also former military heads of state – summarily executed on June 29, 1979. The Rawlings regimes (for he had a second dispensation as perhaps the most reluctant democrat of our rulers) never returned those bodies for burial. It was not until the election of 2000, which brought in the current administration under President John Agyekum Kufuor, that the bodies were exhumed, identified, and returned to their families for interment with the proper rituals. After all I have said, it should be clear how cruelly indecent, what anathema, this defiance of custom had been on the part of the Rawlings administrations. It became a festering example of how, even within our states, some bodies are not legitimate, even in death. Unfortunately, the history of our continent is littered with the bodies of the unburied, unquiet dead. By comparison, the history of Ghana seems a peaceful one. I referred to Rawlings as a reluctant democrat to underscore the truth and the irony that under him we established our Fourth Republic, which has so far seen four relatively peaceful elections, something which none of the first three managed. Thus the poems I am about to share with you must be seen in the context, if you like, of the interregnum that contained our Second and Third Republics and the military regimes that surrounded and interrupted them, in an otherwise comparatively successful attempt to create and secure a legitimate state.

We all knew Afrifa's history, and he remains certainly one of the most controversial leaders, whether seen as a military man or a civilian. Yet his funeral announcement followed the correct conventional format; it gave the dates of his birth and death, followed by the dates of the funeral services, with absolutely no comment whatsoever about the almost twenty-three years in between. What struck me with full force was the ordinariness of what the mourners had done; there was no deviation from the conventional format. It was that simple act that made me realise, with full force, that that is what they had been waiting for two and half decades to do – waiting to bury their dead, simply waiting to perform the last rites for their loved one. It was that lack of comment about the passage of time that made the recognition of its duration so poignant.

The other thing that was self-evident, without comment, after twenty-three years, was the shift in generation of the names of the people making the announcement. They and the chief mourners were no longer principally people of his parents' generation; the principal mourners were now principally the names of his peers, and it was that which also moved me to write the poem for one of those figures, frozen in time, his widow.

And What Remains

For Christine Afrifa,
On the Occasion, After Twenty-Three Years, the Final Funeral
Rites for Her Late Husband

and what remains?
a woman over twenty years his widow, after barely ten years
    his bride;
a life time keeping wake, our dead hero's spirit, restless, by
    her side.

and what remains?
for some of us, the magic heroes of our youth never die;
sometimes they grow up into other selves we do not
    understand,
sometimes they die too young to change,
living in our hearts forever grand,

sometimes, something in between

as, like his orphaned children, we must learn
that to be the hero of one story is to be prepared
to be the villain of another, told by your adversary:
this man was prepared.

The magic almost worked;
the bullets couldn't make him die, at least, not easy, and not
    soon:
such contradictions of torment and triumph
of a life well meant.

and what remains?
to lay to final rest the bones of a man, of soaring restless
    fervour,
and inextinguishable valour.

                           Accra – Ghana, January 2002.

That poem commemorates one of many efforts by the state to bring health unto itself through the ritual forms the society recognises as necessary, a desire for moral health, writ large on the national canvas. Yet it also acknowledges the unspoken, the things that cannot be said over which a narrative of wholeness is attempted – just as the actions of the priestess rituals of remembrance cannot obliterate the past, they can only serve as recompense for that past in communities that accept such ceremonies as recompense. All silences need their witness.

Four years earlier, in the summer of 1998, for the twentieth anniversary of Father's passing at which we unveiled his memorial tombstone, I had written a poem entitled "Of Memory and Loss" in which, once again, I struggled to find the words to speak for the collective group I was representing – in this case my brothers and sisters – and to memorialise our collective history and articulate in poetry the sentiments we all wanted expressed. The point I would like to stress here is that this poem, though intensely personal to us, enters the space of the social as a public text in a political context.

It is the custom in Ghana for the children to unveil the tombstones of their parents on the first anniversary of the death. Thus a delay of twenty years required some explanation, which could not be made without reference to the time of his dying, and the location of his final resting place in his home in Wenchi. The land is the property of his matriclan, bounded on the northeast border by the Wenchi-Akrobi road, the road to his father's home. There are three trees that were important to Father growing up on that property. The first, at the southeast entrance, is the Nyamedua, the sacred tree of the gods, after which the house is named. The second, on the northwest boundary, is a now ageing but once spectacular fan-palm, which when we were young we knew as the tree that ended Nana Abrewa's peanut farm, that great-aunt I spoke of earlier. And the third is to the southwest, on Onyina overlooking the Akrobi road. It was in the shade of this last silk-cotton tree that father, as he often told us, held conversations with his mother and aunt and made all the major decisions of his life, and it was in the shade of this tree that he wished to be buried.

For this reason, when he passed away in Oxford twenty-five years ago, his brothers and sisters determined to bury him there. Our aunts and uncles imagined a straight line between the Nyamedua and the fan-palm, and where that intersected with the line from the silk-cotton to the Akrobi road they dug his grave. In those terrible three weeks – whilst in Accra the then military rulers wrestled, on the one hand, with a family intransigent over the question of granting a state funeral to a man on whose head those self-same rulers had placed a bounty, and on the other, with the executive of his Progress Party determined to bury their founding father in the chiefly manner his life deserved, and while we waited in Oxford for resolutions to these confusions – they quietly cleared the site in Wenchi, dug the grave, and lined it with cement in preparation for the final ceremonies for the familial dead, over which they knew only they had command.

On the day of the burial, after the massed choirs of the Methodist churches from around the country were assembled and singing; and the diplomatic corps were seated, we were sent for. We had been asked to wait until everything was ready in the church, and five minutes before the start of the service we were sent for. As Mama was looking around to check that we were all together, present and ready, we heard the sound of police sirens and turned to see dispatch riders of the military police racing through the gates to halt our progress. They handed our mother a letter whose peremptory instructions have been seared on our memories ever since: "Madam, it has come to our attention that you intend to bury the remains of the late Kofi Busia in the grounds of confiscated property. Under no circumstances is this to be allowed to happen. You are obliged to comply".

In moments of pain and outrage, the most arbitrary things strike our minds. I noticed then that even in death, at the end of a state funeral, they couldn't give our father the respect of a title. Forget "The Right Honourable" to which he had been elected by the overwhelming majority of the people of this country, or even the "Dr." he had earned at such hard cost. He was not even accorded the simple dignity of the "Mr." accorded every mature man and father, let alone one who had helped found a nation. And I noticed above all the cruelty, the lack of simple human compassion in handing a widow a letter written in such a tone, at such a time. They had had weeks to raise the objection. And now, instead of sending someone to explain, or request, someone simply to speak to our mother, they chose to send a messenger with such an outrageous letter, in such a manner, at such a time.

Mother was faced with a choice – to begin a dispute with a functionary, delay the funeral, and turn this most sacred of moments into the occasion of a fiasco and a brawl – or to comply. With characteristic dignity and resolution, after she had calmed the rage of the children, she marshalled some equally appalled bystanders to dig another grave. Some of these men, it must be said to their credit, were also policemen and soldiers who, like their fellows who had helped dig the original grave, had not forgotten simple grace. Mother asked them to have the new place, a piece of garden between the old and the new homes, ready by the time the service was over. This done, we left for the service. Thus the rest of the family was surprised when on returning from the church, we led the pallbearers to a new location.

For twenty years the regional police, who made our home their headquarters, changed guard in front of Papa's grave. For twenty years we, his children, had been determined that we would not raise his tombstone until we could raise it where he had wished to be buried. For twenty years we fought the battle for the restoration of those properties, in order that we might finally lay our father's body to rest. This is a battle we did not win. Representations to successive governments, requests to the Commissioner for Human Rights and Administrative Justice, motions in Parliament, letters and interviews to the press – all had been to no avail. And twenty years had passed. That disruption of the moral universe remained for his siblings, and it remained, as for the families of the executed soldiers, not a private sorrow but a public reproach. Our father, the eldest of thirteen, has only one remaining brother left alive. On the twentieth anniversary, our mother, nearing her eightieth year, and our last paternal uncle made an appeal to us; we had to take counsel. They impressed upon us that for them, this unerected monument represented an unfinished duty of love, and having exceeded their three-score years and ten, they could not be assured of any more decades left. They could not leave this world with our father's tomb still unfinished; what adequate words of explanation could they give? We decided to end our twenty-year silent protest and erected, that year, a memorial where he lay. Still pained by the circumstances, we are assured, however, of two things; first, that for the sake of our mother, our father's remaining brother, and three sisters, we made the kindest decision; and second, that despite these circumstances, we had much to be grateful for. For in the light of the subsequent history of Ghana, the executions of former heads of state, the murders of high court judges, and the acts of violence against ordinary citizens for which we also have had our own Truth Commissions, propitiation must yet be made to set all worlds aright for those to come. We at least do know how and why our father died, and above all, where, indeed, he is buried. Not all the children of people whose parents have played their role in the making of Ghana have been so fortunate. Much has changed, at least on the level of public acts of recompense. The generals have been buried, and though the house in whose shade father wished to be buried has not been restored to us, the one he built in Accra for our mother, who is from Accra, has.

Of Memory and Loss

Beneath God's tree we have kept vigil for two decades:
Injustice leaves turmoil in its wake,
And we still struggle against its tides.

We grow battle weary.

We tell ourselves the dead miss their tombstones
Like sleepers miss the pillows on their beds.
This is not true.

We miss the monuments
As the foundations of our memories crack with time,
And we cling to different fragments of truth.

What is the meaning of death in the face of time?

What lingers always is the memory of loss:
Memorials are the foundations we prepare
To defy the tricks of time.

Elegies are lullabies to rock the already sleeping dead,
Subterfuges for the living; like parents clinging to a child
And singing, long after the infant has been lulled to sleep.

What is the meaning of time in the face of death?

I cling to an anger that will not yield to this truth –
I miss the sound of your laughter, and the touch of your hand.
It is that simple.

Slowly, like falling silk cotton in the wind,
We have found the resolution of a truce:

This should have been a happy song,
But I can't sing in tune,
And I can't sing through tears.

This effort is as hard as the granite we have etched,
Lovingly but war worn, to fulfill our half-kept promise.
We ask your forgiveness.

Slowly, like falling silk cotton in the winds of time,
We have come to revelations:
Beneath God's tree we have kept vigil for two decades:
And the sleep of the Just makes no earthly sound,
So your spirit is quiet:

Because the meaning of death, and the meaning of time,
like the meaning of life, is God's Love.

August 1998.

I marshalled these incidents together out of a faith that poetry anchors us in our sense of being; and that within that poetry, the rituals of mourning in both speech acts and performance, whether formal or informal, demonstrate what is most enduring in us as individuals, and as communities. It is this we can never afford to forget. So I will end with a last poem, called "Achimota", from the story my mother taught me, because I want to bear witness not only to what we know, but how we know it, and how we were made to care. And it is no accident that at the heart of each poem, even if not the subject of the story, the force behind it is a woman. But that is another story.

ACHIMOTA: From The Story My Mother Taught Me

There is a place between Accra and the Legon hills
where they built the famous school.
Everyone thinks of that
today
when the name Achimota
is heard.
Yet the new school takes the name
of the place
but does not reveal what that name means.
The name is A-chi-mo-ta.
It is a forest still, beside the school,
the roads, the railways, and the street side markets.
But the forest came first,
and has always been there.
The trees still stand,
but they do not speak the history they have seen,
A-chi-mo-ta, no, not at all.
And only the name remains the reminder
of who we are, what we have been,
and what we have been through.

Sometimes it seems we are forgetting,
but so long as there are people alive who remember,
we will remember the meaning:
Here we came, fleeing
to a place of shelter,
escaping the chains and lash
we would not submit to,
and these trees hid us.
So, when travelling through
here, searching,
you do not call

by name
in this place.
A-chi-mo-ta,
you do not call,
by name,
out loud,
no, not here.

The underground rail-road had its precursor,
long, long before, on this side of the world.
No one will tell you that today.

We too have been taught forgetting.
We are schooled in another language now
and names lose their meaning except
as labels.
We are being taught forgetting.
But some remember still
Achimota and its history
a forest, and its meaning –
the place, and its silence.

From *Testimonies of Exile*, (Africa World Press),
Trenton NJ, 1990.

(Publisher's note: What is Africa to Me? Is the text of the Mashood Abiola Memorial Lecture delivered by Abena P. A. Busia on November 10, 2005, at a plenary session of the African Studies Association at its Annual Meeting).

References

Apronti, Jawa. 1963. "Funeral." In Gerald Moore and Ulli Beier, eds., *Modern Poetry from Africa*, 104. Baltimore: Penguin Books.
Busia, Abena P. A. 1990. "Exiles", In *Testimonies of Exile*, p.25. Trenton, N.J.: Africa World Press.

Busia, K. A. *The Challenge of Africa*. 1962. New York: Praeger.

Forché, Carolyn. 2000. Introduction to *Against Forgetting: Twentieth-Century Poetry of Witness*. New York: W.W. Norton & Co.

Okpewho, Isidore Oghenerhuele. 1979. *The Epic in Africa: Toward a Poetics of the Oral Performance*. New York: Columbia University Press.

————. 1992. *African Oral Literature: Backgrounds, Character, and Continuity*. Bloomington: Indiana University Press.

————. 1990. ed. *The Oral Performance in Africa*. Ibadan, Nigeria: Spectrum Books.

Soumonni, Eliseé. 2003. "Lacustrine Villages in South Benin as Refuges from the Slave Trade." In Sylviane A. Diouf, ed., *Fighting the Slave Trade: West African Strategies*. Athens: Ohio University Press.

Biographies

Achebe, Chinua
Prominent Nigerian Writer most celebrated for his first classic novel *Things Fall Apart* first published in 1958. This novel, arguably the most widely read work by an African writer has been translated into over 50 languages since it first appeared. Achebe has since gone on to publish over a dozen books including four other novels, collections of poetry in English and Igbo, and many influential essays. He was also the first general editor of the groundbreaking Heinemann African Writers Series, and founded and edited many publications to encourage younger African writers including *Okike*, the journal in which my own poetry first appeared in 1984. This poem, written to honour the golden jubilee of *Things Fall Apart*, during which time it has been continuously in print, opens with an echo of the opening words of celebration of the hero Okonkwo and alludes to the titles of Achebe's other novels and collections of essays.

Afrifa, Akwasi Amankwaa: 24 April 1936–26 June 1979
General Akwasi Amankwa Afrifa is best known as the soldier who, along with Major General Emmanuel Kwasi Kotoka, planned and executed the *coup d'état* against Kwame Nkrumah, Ghana's first President on 24 February 1966. He served as the Head of State himself in the first year of the Second Republic in 1969. A renowned, if controversial, political activist, he actively opposed the regime which toppled the Government of the Second Republic. Arrested and exiled many times as a consequence of his fight for a return to civilian rule, he was executed by Flight Lieutenant Jerry John Rawlings, along with seven other generals, two of whom were also former heads of state, in the turbulence triggered by the 'June 4th' Revolution of 1979. The first poem was written in 1978, shortly after seeing him on his unexpected arrival in England having eluded the military authorities seeking to arrest him.

Afrifa, Christine
Widow of General Akwasi Afrifa, the third Head of State of Ghana, executed by the Rawlings Regime in 1979. The bodies of the 8 people summarily executed on 26 June 1979 were never returned to their families for burial. They were all finally buried in 2001 by the Government of President J. A. Kufuor. This poem was written at the request of Mrs Afrifa to mark the occasion of the burial of her husband, twenty-three years after his execution.

Akoto, Nana Baafuor Osei: 22 February 1904–3 September 2002
Nana Baafour Osei Akoto, Senior Linguist to three successive Asantehenes: namely, Otumfuo Sir Osei Agyeman Prempeh II (1931–9), Otumfuo Opoku Ware II (1970–99), and the current Otumfuo Nana Osei Tutu II. He was a legendary figure in Ghana politics. In addition to his faithful service to the Golden Stool, he is best known for being a founding member of the National Liberation Movement, one of the leading organisations in the struggle for independence which joined with other smaller parties and organisations to form the opposition United Party, under the leadership of Prof. K. A. Busia at the time of Independence. This poem was written as a gift to his son, Dr. Owusu Afriye Akoto, the eighteenth of his thirty-six children, on the occasion of his father's memorial service.

Akufo-Addo, Adeline Sylvia Eugenia Ama Yeboakua: 17 December 1917–21 March 2004
Niece of J. B. Danquah, Sister of William Ofori-Atta, and Wife of Edward Akufo-Addo, (later Chief Justice of the First and President of the Second Republics of Ghana) Adeleine Akufo-Addo had the distinction of being related to three of the 'big six' of Ghana's independence struggles. The daughter of the late Okyehene, Osagyefo Sir Ofori Atta 1, she was the only woman to appear before the 1948 Watson Commission which recommended self-governance for the then British colony. She was the mother of Nana Akufo-Addo, Attorney-General and Minister of Foreign Affairs of the current Fourth republic of Ghana, and the grandmother of Nana Dokua (see below).

Akufo-Addo, Nana Dokua
Granddaughter of Mrs Adeline Akufo-Addo, and daughter of Nana Addo Dankwa Akufo-Addo prominent lawyer and politician who

served as both Attorney general and Minister of Foreign Affairs for the Republic of Ghana. The poem was a birthday present to her on her tenth birthday, the year after the death of her mother, Eleanor Akosua Saah Nkansa Djwamena Akufo-Addo.

Ampah, Joseph Erskine III 24 February 1954–April 27 2006

Ghanaian businessman and friend to paupers, priests and kings alike, who died suddenly at the age of 52 on April 27, 2006. April 27 is South Africa's National Day and I was in Washington DC, a guest of the South African Ambassador Barbara Masekela, the mutual friend who had given me the news when I woke the morning of my own birthday to find the clock frozen at the hour he had passed away, twenty-four hours earlier. Once, when talking about the fact that I wrote mostly narrative free verse, he challenged me by saying: 'Why don't you write a difficult poem, like a haiku or something?' I promised if I ever tried such a thing, the first one I attempted would be for him. I wrote this in the early hours of the morning the day after I learned of his death.

Brodsky, Joseph: 24 May 1940–28 January 1996

Recipient of the Nobel Prize in Literature in 1987, Joseph Brodsky published two plays, several essays and collections of poems in twelve languages. Born in Leningrad, he lived in the United States from 1972, after being exiled from the Soviet Union. By 1992, Brodsky was appointed Poet Laureate of the United States and was Andrew Mellon Professor of Literature at Mount Holyoke College until his death in 1996. The poem was a gift to his widow and inspired by my mother, who knew them, when she heard of his passing. It is centred on the memory of her passionate response to hearing him read his poetry in Russian.

Brown, Wesley

Having earned an MA in Creative Writing and Literature from the City College, CUNY, Wesley Brown taught American Literature, drama and creative writing at Rutgers University from 1979 until he retired in 2005. He has written four plays, *Boogie Woogie and Booker T, Life During Wartime, A Prophet Among Them,* and *Murderess,* published two novels, *Tragic Magic* and *Darktown Strutters* and also co-edited two multicultural anthologies with the late Amy Ling (see below). The poem, composed of the titles of Brown's published creative and critical works, was written as a gift on his retirement from Rutgers University. He is currently working on a collection of short stories entitled *In the Land of Oh-Bla-Dee*.

Bunche, Ralph Johnson: 7 August 1904–9 December 1971

Dr Ralph Bunche, African American educator, political scientist, diplomat and International Civil Servant, was the first person of colour to win the Nobel Peace Prize, in 1950, for negotiating the truce in the Arab-Israeli conflict of 1947. A prominent figure in the Civil Rights movement in the US, Bunche also received the Medal of Freedom from President Lyndon Johnson. He is, however, best remembered around the world for his work at the UN, where he helped draft the original Charter, worked with Eleanor Roosevelt to create and ensure the adoption of the UN Declaration of Human Rights, and for two decades was Director of the Division of Trusteeship. As a trustee, he prepared the international stage for the dozens of nations, particularly in Africa, which gained independence in the two decades following the end of World War II. He died in 1971. I was asked by the organising committee to write the poem for the celebration of the centenary of his birth at his Alma Mater, UCLA, in 2004. The poem makes reference to the bust of him at the entrance to Bunche Hall, overlooking the Sculpture Garden at UCLA, and to Ralph Bunche Park in New York City, opposite the United Nations headquarters; and ends with an echo of the words with which he ended his Nobel Laureate Acceptance Speech: "May there be freedom, equality and brotherhood among all men. May there be morality in the relations among nations. May there be, in our time, at long last, a world at peace in which we, the people, may for once begin to make full use of the great good that is in us."

Busia, Kofi Abrefa: 11 July 1913–28 August 1978

My father, Dr Kofi Abrefa Busia, was a Ghanaian educator, sociologist and statesman. He was Leader of the Opposition at Independence, from 1957-59 and in exile from 1959-66; and served as the only Prime Minister of the Second Republic of Ghana from 1969-72. Busia's career was marked by a number of firsts: before independence, he was the first of two Africans appointed District Commissioner, and the first African to become a professor at the University College of the Gold Coast (now Ghana). Between 1959 and 1966 he taught at universities around the world including Mexico, Oxford and Holland where, at the University of Leiden, he became the first African to hold a university chair in three hundred years, and only the second in its history. Father died during a second period of exile in Oxford, England. The first of the two poems for him was written to alleviate the process of mourning in the three years following his passing; and the second, to commemorate the twentieth anniversary of his passing.

Busia, Kwesi Boaten 20 January 1946–15 May 1974
My cousin, the first-born son of the uncle who followed my father, and his wife, Auntie Mercy Busia, (see below). He trained as a mining engineer in Cornwall, and died suddenly in his sleep at the age of twenty-eight, two weeks after my twenty-first birthday, and two weeks before he was due to return home. This poem, first written as an exercise in a poetry class with Mark Strand at Brandies University the following year, is the first sonnet I ever attempted.

Busia, Mercy Adebi: 11 November 1919–31 May 2007
Mrs Mercy Adebi Busia, was the wife of my Uncle Papa Boaten Busia, the child born after my father, and the mother of my cousin Kwesi Boaten. After briefly running a Dance Academy when studying in England with her husband, she returned to Ghana and served as a social worker, who dedicated her professional life to the welfare of children. She spent many years as the Director of the Osu Children's home. A chance meeting with a stranger at the airport on her way to Norway in 1967 led her to Hermann Gmeiner, the founder of the SOS Children's Villages, in Austria. Impressed by his work, Mercy Busia asked him to build an SOS Children's Village in Ghana and spearheaded the efforts to see the work through. The SOS Children's Village Association of Ghana was founded in 1970, and the first Village opened in 1974. Thirty years after her vision, the Mercy Adebi Busia award was created by SOS in honour of her work; the first award was presented a few weeks after she passed away. I read the poem for her at her funeral service, a few months after her home calling.

Busia, Naa Morkor Abrefa
My mother: one of the first hospital-trained midwives in Ghana, who later trained as teacher when we were in high school in England, she was an artist who created a garden in every home we lived in – in

Ghana, and in the homes of our exiles, especially the one in our child-hood home in England, which she designed from scratch. She is the founder and patron of the Busia Foundation, a Civic Education and charitable organisation founded to commemorate our late father, statesman and Prime Minister of the Second Republic of Ghana, on the twentieth anniversary of his passing. The two poems dedicated to her were written for her seventieth birthday in 1994 and my own fifti-eth in 2003.

Clarke, Nana Ayebia

Nana Ayebia Clarke is a Ghanaian-born Publisher based in Oxfordshire who was the Submissions Editor for Heinemann's African & Caribbean Writers' Series at Oxford and was involved in the publication and promotion of established writers such as Wole Soyinka, Chinua Achebe, Ngugi wa Thiong'o, Nadine Gordimer, Ama Ata Aidoo, Yvonne Vera *et al* for 12 years. She founded Ayebia Clarke Publishing Ltd in 2003 as a way of looking to new directions after Heinemann's decision to cease the publication of new titles in the African Writers' Series in 2002. Under the Ayebia imprint, she has reissued *Nervous Conditions* (2004) by Tsitsi Dangarembga and the sequel to her award-winning novel entitled *The Book of Not* (2006), *The Cry of Winnie Mandela* (2004) by Njabulo S. Ndebele, Lewis Nkosi's *Underground People* (2005), Ken Saro-Wiwa's *A Month and A Day & Letters* (2005), *Between Faith & History: A Biography of President J. A. Kufuor* by Ivor Agyeman-Duah (2006) and *The Legacy of Efua Sutherland* (2007) co-edited by Anne V. Adams and Esi Sutherland-Addy *et al*.

I was introduced to Nana Ayebia by Professor Ama Ata Aidoo in November 2000 at a seminar in Accra during the week of the Ghana International Book Fair. Although we had not met previously, we shared a common friend – and one of Ayebia's treasured editors from her Heinemann days – Penny Ormerod who was at St Anne's College, Oxford, with me. So our first meeting was an incredible co-incidence since Nana Ayebia (herself an Oxford graduate) said she had heard a lot about me from Penny and felt she knew me well.

Nana Ayebia is responsible for two of the pieces in this collection; *Between Faith & History* was written for the launch of President Kufuor's biography which I read at the event in Accra on 10 January 2007. I had come home to Ghana in the summer of 2008 to care for my ailing Mother and wondered if I had taken on too much by promising to write a piece for Efua Sutherland. Nana Ayebia instinctively informed me that she felt it is essential to include a piece for Sutherland and that she was prepared to extend the deadline to enable me to do this.

Coffin, Reverend William Sloane, Jr: 1 June 1924–19 April 2006

Internationally known, inspirational Christian clergyman and long-time peace activist, Reverend Coffin was the Senior Minister of the Riverside Church in the City of New York at the time I joined the church in the early 1980s. Before his ordination he prepared for a career as a concert pianist, and worked as a CIA agent in his early years. That experience left him severely disillusioned with the role the US government had played in post-war International affairs, and he became one of the most ardent Peace Activists of his age, protesting against every US military intervention from Vietnam to Iraq, from his pulpits, on the streets, and in whatever peaceful media he could find, until the day he died. He was equally active in the Civil Rights and Human Rights movements, within and outside the US, including the anti-Apartheid struggle in South Africa. As Chaplain at Yale University, he organised 'freedom rides' to challenge segregation in the South, and at Riverside he declared the church a sanctuary for refugees from Central America, and hosted Nelson Mandela on his release from prison. He resigned from Riverside Church to become President of SANE/Freeze (now Peace Action), the nation's largest peace and justice group, in 1987; and the poem, inspired by two of his sermons, including the one he preached on the difficulty of making that decision, was my gift to him at his retirement party.

Essandoh, Louis Kofi

Dr Louis Essandoh graduated from the Yale School of Medicine in 1981 where he specialised in Cardiology, and did his residency at the celebrated Mayo Clinic in Rochester MN. In private practice in Maryland, he is also a research Professor at Johns Hopkins University. He is married to my cousin Nana Frema the daughter of Nana Kusi Apea, one of my father's younger brothers, and the poem was written to be read at the ceremony when he was honoured by the American Heart Association of Anne Arundel County MD, in April 2001.

Friedman, Peggy: 18 August 1949–8 February 2006
Professor of History Alan Howard and his then fiancée, Peggy
Friedman, were amongst the first friends I made when I joined the
faculty at Rutgers University in the early 1980s. Peggy was an instruc-
tor for many years in the English and Comparative Literature
departments. Growing up in Belgium and the Netherlands, she was a
multi-linguist who taught English in various countries. She also
played a role as a political activist on both local and global issues,
particularly those involving education and human rights. She died
after a long and valiant struggle against cancer in February 2006, and
the poem containing references to her writing assignments and
moments that I shared with her over two decades, was written to be
read for me by fellow poet and Rutgers colleague Cheryl Clarke, at
her memorial service a few weeks later. I last saw her at the funeral
service for Toby Schroeder (see below) a few days before leaving for
a sabbatical in Accra where I was when I got the news of her death.

Johnson, Lemuel: 1941–12 March 2002
Born and educated in both Sierra Leone and the United States,
Lemuel Johnson served as a professor of English at the University of
Michigan, Ann Arbor, from 1968 until his death in 2002, and was
Director of the Center for African and African American Studies there
between 1985 and 1991. A distinguished poet and author of ten books,
including his highly acclaimed *Sierra Leone Trilogy* of poems, Johnson,
who spoke ten languages, was also an award-winning teacher and
much beloved mentor of many people. He served as the President of
the African Literature Association in 1977-78, and Vice-President of
the Caribbean Studies Association from 1983-85. I was one of many
people he mentored. The letter was written to him posthumously for
the celebration of his life held at his university, two years after his
passing, recalls at random a series of shared conversations, current
events, works read in common, joyous dances with him at ALA
parties, and an acknowledgement of his early support for the *Women
Writing Africa* project whose second volume was in process at the time
of writing.

Kellerman, Lynne A: 11 August 1947–06 December 1986
My friend Lynne M. Kellermann began her career at Livingston
College at Rutgers as a secretary and earned her BA, and MA, in

English Literature and Specialists Degree in Education at Rutgers University while working in various capacities. She taught in the writing programme at Livingston, and I worked closely with her for my first five years when she became director of the college's Honours programme, a position she held until her untimely death from cancer in 1986. This poem, made up of fragments of my journal entry and recollections of my last conversation with her was written for her memorial service at Rutgers shortly after she died.

Kufuor, John Agyekum

President of the Republic of Ghana from 2000-2008, was born in Kumasi into a distinguished ancient Ashanti family of wealthy chiefs and warriors, with a long tradition of service and leadership. A lawyer by training, he also studied Politics, Philosophy and Economics at Exeter College, Oxford University. He became at 28 the youngest legal advisor at the now Kumasi Metropolitan Authority (Ghana's second largest city), and subsequently Member of Parliament, and Deputy Minister of Foreign Affairs at 30 under the Government of his mentor, my father, Prof. K. A. Busia. He was arrested and jailed for a year after the *coup d'etat* that toppled that government of the Second Republic of Ghana. Seven years later he was back in parliament as the Opposition spokesperson for Foreign Affairs during the Third Republic. He was the defeated presidential candidate of the NPP in the 1996 elections before leading his party twice to victory in 2000 and in 2004. The poem was written at the request of publisher Nana Ayebia Clarke and was read at the Accra launch of *Between Faith and History: A Biography of J. A. Kufuor* by Ivor Agyeman-Duah, on January 10, 2007.

Lennon, John Winston Ono: 9 October 1940–8 December 1980

John Lennon, singer, songwriter, political activist and member of The Beatles, with Paul McCartney formed one of the most influential and creative song-writing partnerships of the twentieth century. He was murdered by Mark David Chapman on arriving home at the 'Dakota' Apartments in NYC after leaving a recording session with his wife, Yoko Ono. This poem, written on the day he died, is one of only two in the anthology written to someone I never personally knew or met. It is more than anything else an elegy for my lost childhood in an English country village.

Ling, Amy: 28 May 1939–21 August 1999

Amy Ling, my friend and former colleague at Rutgers University ended her long, path-breaking career as the Director of the Asian American Studies programme at the University of Wisconsin, Madison, from 1991 until her death in 1999. She worked tirelessly to establish the field of Asian American Studies as a discipline in the United States, and was honoured for her contributions with Lifetime Achievement Awards from the Society for the Study of Multiethnic Literature of the United States (1997) and the Asian American Studies Association (2000). She wrote and edited numerous books on Asian American and multicultural literature including the two anthologies *Imagining America* and *Visions of America*, with Wesley Brown (see above). Amy Ling died after a long battle with cancer, and the poem, written for her memorial service at Rutgers, commemorates the last time I saw her, on my wedding day some fifteen months before; and the gift she brought me on that day, when she stopped over in NJ to attend the ceremony en route back home to Madison from Italy.

Lorde, Audre Geraldine: 18 February 1934–7 November 1992

Audre Lorde, an influential poet, labour activist, writer, cultural worker and cancer survivor, known for her passionate politics in the gay rights and lesbian feminist movements. A founder of the Kitchen Table: Women of Color Press, and a prolific writer who published thirteen books of poetry, essays and autobiography, Lorde used her 'sister outsider' status to challenge sexism and racism, in particular the racism of feminism in the United States. An inspiration to a generation of women writers of colour, the former Poet Laureate of New York and self-described 'black lesbian, mother, warrior, and poet' lost her battle against breast cancer in 1992. I am one of a younger generation of poets whose work she encouraged and promoted. At her request, I performed at the Sister to Sister conference organised in her honour in October 1990. The poem 'I am your sister' was written as a gift of healing after a painful moment of misunderstanding on the first night of the conference, and the 'Lamentation' was written for the celebration of her life held at Rutgers two years later, shortly after her death.

Mandela, Nelson Rolihlahla

The most famous political prisoner of the twentieth century, Nelson Rolihlahla Mandela, was an Anti-Apartheid freedom fighter and prisoner who lived to become the first democratically elected President of a free South Africa, from 1994 to 1999. He became the leader of *Umkhonto we Sizwe*, the military wing of the African National Congress when, after the Sharpeville massacre in 1960, it abandoned its policy of non-violence. Mandela was arrested in August 1962 on charges of incitement and leaving South Africa without valid travel documents. He was subsequently sentenced to life imprisonment with hard labour at the end of the Rivonia trial. Mandela served twenty-seven years in prison, 1962-90, much of it in solitary confinement. This poem was written in the early hours of the morning of 11 February 1990 while awaiting his imminent release from prison, and read to him as part of the festivities he attended in Los Angeles on 29 June 1990, a few months after his release. After his release, he won many accolades and awards, including the Nobel Peace Prize which he shared with F. W. de Klerk in 1993. Now considered an international elder statesman, on his eighty-ninth birthday, he helped found an organisation known as Global Elders, a group of twelve statesmen who evaluate and offer assistance to tackle prevailing global problems. The group includes Kofi Annan, Desmond Tutu, Gro Harlem Brundtland, former presidents Mary Robinson, and Jimmy Carter, Li Zhaoxing, Muhammad Yunus, Ela Bhatt, Gracia Machel, and, of course, Nelson Mandela himself.

Montreal Massacre Martyrs–6 December 1989

This poem honours the fourteen women who died in the Montreal Massacre of 6 December 1989. These women, Geneviève Bergeron, 21; Hélène Colgan, 23; Nathalie Croteau, 23; Barbara Daigneault, 22; Anne-Marie Edward, 21; Maud Haviernick, 29; Barbara Maria Klucznik, 31; Maryse Leclair, 23; Annie St-Arneault, 23; Michèle Richard, 21; Maryse Laganière, 25; Anne-Marie Lemay, 22; Sonia Pelletier, 28; and Annie Turcotte, 21, were all students at The Ecole Polytechnique in Montreal. They were shot in a killing spree by Marc Lépine who proclaimed that as engineering students, they were feminists and feminists had ruined his life. The poem was first written and first read on behalf of the Rutgers University Center for Women's Global Leadership at a memorial service organised by the Canadian Embassy in Accra, Ghana on 6 December 1995, to commemorate the 16 Days of Activism against Gender Violence which the Center has facilitated since it initiated and organised the first one in 1991. Beginning on 25 November, International Day Against Violence

Against Women and ending on 10 December, International Human Rights Day, this sixteen-day period which links women's rights to human rights includes 29 November, International Women Human Rights Defenders Day; 1 December, World AIDS Day; in addition to 6 December, the Anniversary of the Montreal Massacre.

Nkiado, Miriam

I know almost nothing about Miriam Nkiado, (not even the correct spelling of her name which could also be rendered Nkeado: she is Gonja and the spoken name can be spelled either way) except what I learned, travelling with a group of NJ educators on a Fulbright-Hays project along the internal slave routes of Ghana and Benin. We had a chance encounter with her tending her crops by an ancient tree. When asked who she was and what she was doing, what she said to us was the inspiration for the poem. When asked why she continued the service she did, she replied that all people are human, and had their people known of their deaths they would have done something; but they did not know, so it is those of us who do know who must perform what rites we can and in the shadow of that tree is where they died, so it is there she must do her work. As she was trained by her aunt, she is training her niece to continue the tradition.

Nyerere, Julius Kambarage: 13 April 1922–14 October 1999

A teacher and political activist, Julius Nyerere formed the Tanganyika African National Union as a means of uniting multiple national factions to fight for the independence of his country. He was elected first as Prime Minister, then as President, when Tanganyika gained its full independence in 1961, and became President of the United Republic of Tanzania on the Union of Tanganyika and Zanzibar in 1964. Nyerere proposed several solutions to develop the economy of his country, and his theory of Collective Socialism or *Ujamaa* made him a household name in Africa. He voluntarily stepped out of office, after serving as Head of State from 1961-85. Winner of the 1987 Lenin Peace Prize, Nyerere spent his later years in various capacities, including as the emissary of peace during the Burundi conflict of 1996. He died of leukemia in 1999. I had the honour of meeting him on two occasions after his retirement, and the poem was written for the memorial tribute organised by the African Studies Association the month after he died.

Olympio, Alero: 31 May 1959–23 August 2005
Alero Olympio was a talented architect who practised in Edinburgh, Scotland and Ghana. Well known for a diverse array of work, she championed the use of laterite as building material for contemporary African architecture. After battling cancer for six years, she died at the age of 46. The poem was written for a private commemoration of her life, held at the Kokrobitey Institute, one of her signature architectural projects in Accra, Ghana in January 2006.

Schroeder, Toby Lund: 7 March 2001–3 December 2005
Younger son of my friends and colleagues at Rutgers University, Dorothy Hodgson and Rick Schroeder, who died suddenly at the age of four when with his parents on their research leave in Arusha, Tanzania. The poem, centred on the meanings of their respective names, was written as a gift for his parents and elder brother Luke, and read at his memorial service at Rutgers University a few weeks after his passing.

Streetman, Chic and Karen Sorensen
Chic Street Man, acoustic blues musician, composer, and educator, best known in theatre circles for composing the music and starring in the off-Broadway hit show, *Spunk*, adapted by George C. Wolfe from three short stories by Zora Neale Hurston; and being the composer, arranger and Music Director and performer in *Polk County*, the unpublished play by Hurston, which he helped bring to the stage for the first time in 2002. Streetman's career, however, has been long and varied, having worked as a psychodramatist in a Community Hospital, and run his own performing arts school. He is most in demand internationally as a solo performer and cultural worker who uses his music to teach about and fight for human rights, peace and justice; a vocation which has earned him the title of 'UN Musical Ambassador for Peace and Human Rights'. The poem was the gift he asked for, for not being able to attend his wedding. He married musician Karen Sorensen in Seattle Washington on 2 October 1993 the same day as I had already promised to be at the wedding of other friends of mine in Annapolis MD.

Stuckey, Sterling

Historian Professor P. Sterling Stuckey spent most of his academic career at his Alma Mater, Northwestern University from 1971 to 1989, and then at UC Riverside until his retirement as UC President's Chair in 2004. Stuckey's 1968 article 'Through the prism of Folklore: the Black Ethos in Slavery' (and *Slave Culture* his 1987 book, which grew out of it), is today regarded as one of the most influential articles published on the question of slave culture. By making Africans central in America as agents in their own lives, it shifted the paradigms of how historical research itself could be done. A scholar of intellectual and cultural history, his works, ranging from books and articles on Paul Robeson and Herman Melville to African American Art, have influenced a generation of scholars like myself, in all disciplines, interested in the enduring impact of the African American presence on American life. I was asked by Professors Robert Hill and Michael Gomez, two of his distinguished former students, to write and perform the poem for the celebration of his life and work at the conference they organised in his honour at his retirement from UC Riverside. This is a poem woven of references to his body of work and interests from, Sprituals to Civil Rights.

Sutherland, Efua Theodora: 27 June 1924–21 January 1996

Efua Theodora Sutherland (née Morgue), Ghanaian playwright, poet and children's author helped to establish the literary magazine *Okyeame* and Afram Publications and is credited with being the founder of or inspiration behind such present institutions in Ghana as the Ghana Society of Writers, the Ghana Experimental Theatre and the Ghana Drama Studio, (now Writers' Workshop in the Institute of African Studies), the Kodzidan (Story House) in Ekumfi-Atiwa and the biennial PANAFEST festival of Pan-African theatre and drama. As such she is a towering figure in the establishment of modern Ghanaian theatre, and as a research fellow in literature and drama at the Institute of African Studies at the University of Ghana, helped to establish the study of African performance traditions as worthy of university level study. In her final years she established the Mmofra Foundation to support creative work in the arts, particularly those in indigenous languages, for the benefit of children. Her life-long work for children and the arts is continued by her three children Esi Sutherland-Addy, Ralph Sutherland, and Amowi Sutherland-Phillips through the work of this foundation. She passed away in Accra on January 21st 1996, the very day of her last-born child's 39th birthday. The singularly important first anniversary of her death thus fell on Amowi's 40th birthday. For this reason, contrary to Ghanaian tradition which generally commemorates people on the day they died, the family holds the public rituals of remembrance for the life of Auntie Efua, (who was the aunt of my sister-in-law Dinah), every year on the day of her own birth, June 27th, instead.

Windle, Ariana Worthington Clarke: 2 October 1951–30 August 2004

A friend who lived in Standlake, the English country village outside Oxford in which I lived with my family as a child, Ariana Windle was a painter who worked primarily in pastels, and a community art teacher who worked with pensioners and children to create several public art projects made of mosaics made from found and recycled materials. One of her most familiar local projects was the mosaic goose on the village green, and a tryptich on the River Windrush, opposite Standlake Village Church, dedicated in her honour. Her daughter Christina called me to give me the news of her death on what was, for me, the first day of the new school year. The structure of the poem came to me a week later when, impeded by a large funeral cortège from getting to the parking lot of my office, I circled the streets of New Brunswick grieving that I could not be at her funeral which was to take place in Standlake the following day. I read it at the memorial service for her the following month in her birthplace, Clarksville VA.

Yergan, Max: 19 July 1894–12 April 1975

Max Yergan was an early African American Civil Rights activist, whose career swung the political spectrum in the United States from working with Paul Robeson to co-found the International Committee (later Council) on African Affairs in 1937, to being a staunch Anti-Communist Cold Warrior in the last years of his life. Such is the complexity of views surrounding him that despite being a mentor to Govan Mbeki, one of the 'Rivonia Eight' tried and sentenced with Mandela in 1964, Yergan could still be accused of being an apologist for apartheid South Africa. Though little remembered in the US, Yergan has had a lasting institutional impact in South Africa, where in 1920 he was the first African American to go to work as a Baptist missionary and social worker for the YMCA. He was instrumental in founding the Jan H. Hofmeyr School of Social Work in Johannesburg, where a range of influential people from Southern Africa including Joshua Nkomo, Eduardo Mondlane, Ellen Kuzwayo, and Winnie Madikizela-Mandela received their training. On returning to the United States, Dr Yergan became the first African American faculty member ever hired at City College in New York, teaching the course 'Negro History and Culture' in the fall of 1937, so creating one of the very first courses taught in the country on this subject. He was later denied reappointment, and dismissed for his political views. I first met him in 1962 during our first exile, when our family moved from Holland to Mexico via New York. He was one of the people who supported my father in his efforts to secure the release of colleagues detained by Nkrumah, or exiled though opposition to the CPP (Convention Peoples' Party – Nkrumah's Party) in the 1960s. Dr Yergan died in 1975, when I was spending a year away from Oxford at Brandeis University in the US. His was the first funeral I ever recall attending and the poem records what we did on the day.